The U.S.S.R. and Global Interdependence

The U.S.S.R. and Global Interdependence

Alternative Futures

Walter C. Clemens, Jr.

American Enterprise Institute for Public Policy Research
Washington, D. C.

Walter C. Clemens, Jr., is professor of political science at Boston University and an associate of the Russian Research Center at Harvard University.

Library of Congress Cataloging in Publication Data

Clemens, Walter C
The U.S.S.R. and global interdependence.

(AEI studies ; 190)
Includes bibliographic references and index.
1. Russia—Foreign relations—1975– I. Title.
II. Series: American Enterprise Institute for Public Policy Research. AEI studies ; 190.
JX1555.Z5 1978 327.47 78-7666
ISBN 0-8447-3292-3

AEI studies 190

Printed in the United States of America

for
W.E.L.

CONTENTS

ACKNOWLEDGMENTS

The author wishes to thank the following organizations for sponsoring portions of this research: Boston University; the Rockefeller Foundation; the Villa Serbelloni; the U.S. Department of State through a grant to the Harvard University Russian Research Center; the Kennan Institute for Advanced Russian Studies, the Woodrow Wilson International Center for Scholars, the Smithsonian Institution; and the American Enterprise Institute for Public Policy Research.

S. Frederick Starr, secretary of the Kennan Institute, James H. Billington, director of the Woodrow Wilson Center, and Samuel F. Wells, Jr., secretary, International Security Studies at the Wilson Center, and many other colleagues at the Wilson Center have facilitated the study significantly. Vladimir Brovkin, now of Princeton University, and A. James Melnik, formerly of Harvard University, have provided many stimulating ideas as well as valuable research assistance.

Collaboration with other colleagues at the Harvard Russian Research Center—Helen Desfosses, Robert Legvold, Sarah M. Terry, William Taubman, Vladimir I. Toumanoff, and Angela S. and Daniel Yergin—has been rewarding, both personally and professionally. John P. Hardt of the Library of Congress and Robert J. Pranger of the American Enterprise Institute provided helpful critiques of a first draft of the study. Valuable suggestions have also been made by Kendall E. Bailes, University of California, Irvine; Abraham Brumberg, Department of State; Vera S. Dunham, Queens College; Nikolai N. and Margarita Inozemtsev, Institute of International World Economics and International Relations (IMEMO), Moscow; George F. Kennan, Princeton University; Steven Rosefielde, University of North Carolina; John R. Thomas, National Science Foundation; Judith A. Thornton,

University of Washington; and Alexander Yanov, University of California, Berkeley.

Anne E. Griesse of Georgetown University has performed beyond the call of duty in checking citations and preparing the manuscript for publication. Eloise Doane of the Wilson Center gracefully supervised its typing.

The author, as well as the subject, is globally interdependent, but is glad for it.

Black Rock, Tobago
April 1978

1
Introduction

In place of the old local and national seclusion and self-sufficiency, we have intercourse in every direction, universal interdependence of nations. And as in material, so also in intellectual production.

KARL MARX, 1848

Defining the Issues

Interdependence or security? The major issues of Soviet foreign policy since Stalin's death contribute to this dilemma and bear on its resolution: Arms race or arms control with Washington? Forward strategy in the Third World or quietism? Reinforcement of the Iron Curtain or security agreements and economic collaboration with the West? Hostile relations with Peking or a *modus vivendi*? Retention of a siege mentality and a zero-sum approach to world affairs or a serious attempt to cope with escalating interdependencies in a spirit of mutual aid?

What do we mean by "interdependence"? Transactions across national frontiers have been rising at a rapid rate for decades, but interdependence is more than interconnectedness.[1] It is a relationship in which the well-being (welfare, security, or other) of two or more actors is sensitive or vulnerable to changes in the condition or policies

---

Karl Marx, *Communist Manifesto* (1848). Though this English translation was approved by Engels, the German reads "general [all-sided] dependence of nations upon each other" (*An die Stelle der alten lokalen und nationalen Selbstgenügsamkeit und Abgeschlossenheit tritt ein allseitiger Vehrkehr, eine allseitge Abhängigkeit der Nationen voneinander.*) The Russian comes closer to the German: *Prikhodit . . . vsestoronnaia zavisimost' natsii drug ot druga.* "Interdependence" in German would be *gegenseitige Abhängigkeit*; in Russian, *vzaimozavisimost'*. "Dependence upon each other" or "mutual dependence" could imply a relationship less symmetrical and organic than theoretically perfect "interdependence."

[1] According to Alex Inkeles, many forms of human interconnectedness across national frontiers have doubled every ten years in recent decades. See his "The Emerging Social Structure of the World," *World Politics*, no. 27 (July 1975), pp. 467–95 at p. 479.

of the other.[2] It is a point along a spectrum ranging from the absolute independence of each actor, at one extreme, to the absolute dependence of one, at the other.[3] Though interdependence may entail mutual benefit, the costs of changing the relationship may be measured in terms of mere sensitivity or deep vulnerability: "Sensitivity means liability to costly effects imposed from outside . . . before any policies are devised to try to change the situation. Vulnerability means continued liability to costly effects imposed from outside, even after efforts have been made to alter or escape the situation."[4]

Some actors and analysts may perceive certain interdependencies as zero-sum, negative-sum, or positive-sum, but the realities of world politics are generally variable-sum, with a potential—as in the game of Prisoner's Dilemma—to beggar one's neighbor or, alternatively, to optimize common interests.[5]

Relationships of interdependence may be asymmetrical or symmetrical. They may result from conscious choice, coercion, or unforeseen developments; they may be unidimensional, focused on one central relationship, or complex, ranging across many dimensions; they may be short-term or long-term in character. Finally, they may exist objectively, without being perceived, or vice versa.

Soviet writers have generally stressed that Western statements about interdependence originated in Washington's search for an ideo-

---

[2] Though the present discussion of world affairs is focused on "international actors"—states, international organizations, multinational corporations, transnational movements—study of dependencies among other actors—spouses, parents and children, competing firms, even man and nature—may yield fruitful insights. See, for example, the discussion of social symbioses in Edward O. Wilson, *Sociobiology: The New Synthesis* (Cambridge, Mass.: Harvard University Press, Belknap Press, 1975), pp. 353ff.

[3] Beyond interdependence is *integration,* a condition in which formerly autonomous units have surrendered many vital functions to another, more extended unit; integration by force is *hegemony.* Though integration sometimes presupposes or leads to similarities of societal organization, one cannot speak of *convergence* unless two or more units gravitate toward a common form along some dimension—sociopolitical structure, for example. See Inkeles, "The Emerging Social Structure of the World," pp. 471–72.

[4] Joseph S. Nye, "Independence and Interdependence," *Foreign Policy,* no. 22 (Spring 1976), pp. 129–61 at p. 133; for a fuller discussion, see Robert O. Keohane and Joseph S. Nye, *Power and Interdependence* (Boston: Little, Brown & Company, 1977), especially pp. 8–17. For other important studies and bibliographical references, see also Richard Rosecrance and Arthur Stein, "Interdependence: Myth or Reality?" *World Politics,* vol. 26, no. 1 (October 1973), pp. 1–27; Hayward R. Alker, Jr., Lincoln P. Bloomfield, Nazli Choucri, *Analyzing Global Interdependence,* 4 vols. (Cambridge, Mass.: M.I.T. Center for International Studies, 1974).

[5] See Steven J. Brams, *Game Theory and Politics* (New York: Macmillan Company, The Free Press, 1975), pp. 26–46.

logical fig leaf to cover its hegemonistic designs over Western Europe in the 1950s and, in the 1970s, over the Third World.[6] In the mid-1970s, Soviet analysts note, Western writers have also begun to speak of interdependence between capitalist and socialist countries. And one Soviet analyst has traced bourgeois theorizing back to the "repository of theoretical constructions of the American sociologist Talcott Parsons, who had referred to the 'interdependence' of the different components of bourgeois society—the social strata and classes—in characterizing its social structure."[7]

Soviet writers began in the mid-1970s, as we shall see, to find the origins of the concept of interdependence in Lenin's concept of a system of states and to distinguish between policies of "sham" and "genuine" interdependence. Few, however, seem to have noticed the quotation from the *Communist Manifesto* cited above which, if not an accurate description of the mid-nineteenth century, accurately forecast world trends in the latter half of the twentieth.

Whether or not mutual vulnerabilities and sensitivities between East and West are fully recognized, and regardless of how they are labeled, they have existed for years, and they are steadily becoming more important, even if perceptions lag realities. The sources of Soviet interdependence with the Western world, but especially the United States, in the 1970s are outlined in Table 1, their salience ranked from left to right. Thus, the overriding issue for both Moscow and Washington is the fact that each country's survival is hostage to the other's forbearance. They have recognized their mutual vulnerability in the 1972 treaty, renouncing—at least for the present—any effort to build large-scale antiballistic missile defenses.[8] The domestic security of the Soviet Union and the external security as well are vulnerable to Western policies. Soviet sensitivity has exisited for decades (witness Kremlin efforts to jam Western broadcasts and limit circulation of Western publications), but the potential for Western policies to push Moscow's internal problems over a critical

[6] A Soviet book published in 1975 traces American use of *interdependence* to dominate Europe to John Foster Dulles in 1958. It asserts that President de Gaulle correctly assessed the U.S. formula as a device to maintain American colonial hegemony over Europe. See A. E. Efremov, *Evropeiskaia bezopasnost' i krizis NATO* (Moscow: Nauka, 1975), pp. 73–74.

[7] A. Sergiyev, "Bourgeois Theories of 'Interdependence' Serve Neocolonialism," *International Affairs*, no. 11 (November 1976), pp. 103–11 at p. 104. "The class meaning of Parsons' theory," Sergiyev holds, "was maintenance of the balance between the bourgeoisie and the working class by the latter renouncing the class struggle."

[8] In 1974 both sides agreed to limit themselves to just one ABM site with no more than 100 launchers.

TABLE 1
SOURCES OF SOVIET-U.S. INTERDEPENDENCE

High ← *Dominance-ranking of issue areas* → *Low*

	Military Security	Political Security[a]	Economic Well-being	Scientific and Technological Transfer	Environmental Protection	Cultural Transfer
Asymmetry ↔ *Symmetry*	joint vulnerability	Soviet vulnerability	Soviet sensitivity	Soviet sensitivity	joint sensitivity	joint sensitivity

Low ← *Complexity of interdependence among instruments and dimensions of cooperation and competition* → *High*

See notes to table on p. 5.

threshold has increased in the 1970s because of the mounting strength of Soviet dissident movements. Moscow's ability to exert comparable pressures in the West is quite low, the strength of Eurocommunism deriving almost entirely from endogenous factors.

In recent years the Kremlin has looked increasingly to the West for trade and transfer of technology to inject new life into the sluggish Soviet economy. The economy of the Soviet Union is not yet vulnerable (in the strict sense used above) to changes in Western policies, but it is becoming more and more sensitive. Though individual firms in the West may be sensitive or even vulnerable to Soviet practices, the United States and most other Western national economies are not heavily dependent on the U.S.S.R. The environmental well-being of all countries, including the Soviet Union, is sensitive both to the waste and to the technological progress of the United States and Western Europe. But both East and West have much to learn from each other and have gained considerably from joint environmental projects in recent years. The same is true in the realm of cultural exchange, though the most powerful influences—Soviet artists emigrating to the West, and Western music surmounting Soviet-made barricades—have probably had their effects against the Kremlin's will.

Soviet-American relations thus fall somewhere between the polar visions of traditional realists and contemporary transnationalists.[9] The former see world politics as dominated by monolithic actors trying to maximize power and putting a premium on force as a way to obtain their objectives. The latter perceive a complex interdependence in which heterogeneous actors communicate by means of multiple

---

NOTE to Table 1, p. 4: This table should be compared with two similar ones in Robert O. Keohane and Joseph S. Nye, *Power and Interdependence* (Boston: Little, Brown & Company, 1977), pp. 17, 217, where they include also the elements of cost-ranking (military higher than others) and comparative social distance among nations. The U.S.-U.S.S.R. dyad is probably closer in terms of social distance (cultural and historical considerations) than, say, the United States (or the Soviet Union) with China or Nigeria, but not so close as U.S. relations with most NATO countries or some East European states, such as Poland or Czechoslovakia. The extent of this distance (or closeness, depending on one's standard for measurement) affects the manner in which these sources of interdependence are perceived in both countries.

[a] The security of the regime is probably more important to the leaders of the CPSU than is the security of the state (inviolability of frontiers, for example), but Washington's ability to undermine the regime is far less than the U.S. threat to Soviet state security interests. Leaders in both countries are probably tempted to place their own short-range political strength over the economic well-being of the country as a whole.

[9] These poles are aptly presented by Keohane and Nye in *Power and Interdependence*, pp. 24ff, who also make a case for a synthesis dependent upon the context of time and place.

channels on a wide variety of issues (many of them more relevant if not more weighty than security) and use a wide variety of instrumentalities, from economic incentives to consensus building in the United Nations. In a confrontation such as the Cuban missile crisis, security considerations are paramount for both superpowers; in the allocation of resources for the bilateral relationship, military security gets by far the greatest share (though it is outweighed, at least within the United States, by expenditures on welfare and on education). The day-to-day agenda of the two countries, however, even if dominated by military considerations, also includes many political, economic, scientific-technological, environmental, and cultural issues in which military force is not a relevant or usable arbiter.

In truth, we can speak of a world of escalating interdependencies, with the superpowers leading the way, particularly in the realm of strategic affairs, each becoming steadily more vulnerable to the other. What to do about this situation is another question, for "interdependence" describes the world but does not dictate the most rational or feasible response to this condition. And though the assets and liabilities of each side may be reflected in Table 1, this listing only approximates initial bargaining positions. It does not predetermine what use each side may make of its capacities. As always, skill, determination, and chance will be critical to the shaping of decisions and outcomes. Whether each side will perceive its own interests accurately, much less act wisely on them, remains to be seen. The thrust of the present analysis is to suggest that, while each side may score short-term gains by exploiting the other's vulnerabilities and sensitivities, the long-term interests of most citizens—East and West—are most likely to be served by explicit recognition of their interdependencies and the forging of cooperative strategies designed to optimize common goals in the realms of peace and economic and environmental well-being.

Defining the Tendencies

Attitudes toward interdependence and security in the U.S.S.R., as in other countries, are complex, shifting, and far from monolithic. They reflect the personal values and experiences of diverse individuals, their institutional concerns, and domestic and external conditions as perceived by these individuals. These perceptions, in turn, reflect the impact of culture, history, and ideology as assimilated in the personal makeup of different observers.[10]

---

[10] For elaboration, see, for example, Walter C. Clemens, Jr., *The Arms Race and Sino-Soviet Relations* (Stanford, Calif.: Hoover Institution, 1968), pp. 231–39.

How many tendencies or schools exist on questions of interdependence versus security? The number and type could range as high as the membership of the Politburo or even the entire Central Committee, along with every KGB official, dissident, journalist, academician, or factory manager with views on this subject. Alternatively, we could reduce all contending forces to one or more pairs of polar opposites.[11] The problem is to identify and utilize models which, though simplified, help us to understand a complex reality.

We distinguish here four basic tendencies—détente and trade, globalism, forward strategy, and autarky (each with important subgroups)—plus a mixed model. This delineation derives from a combination of logical alternatives, consideration of historical patterns, and analysis of Soviet statements.[12] A much larger number would become unmanageable and violate parsimony; a smaller number—especially if it focused on polar opposites—would oversimplify the multifaceted character and emphases of Soviet thinking.[13]

In the U.S.S.R., as in other countries, private and official views concerning interdependence have evolved rapidly since the early 1970s and are still in flux. The four viewpoints sketched here should be regarded as tendencies more than as fixed schools. In practice, as suggested below, all four approaches may be pursued concurrently.

We cannot expect to find schools of thought contending so openly in the U.S.S.R. as in the West. Only the current official line favored by dominant figures within the Politburo may be directly expressed without hesitation. If the top leaders disagree, of course, they may make public speeches—Brezhnev on the inexhaustibility of Soviet resources; Kosygin on their limitations—and both may be reported, sometimes with no attempt to mask contradictory passages.[14] There is also an important difference between Brezhnev's vigorous endorsements since 1971 of "long-term, large-scale economic cooperation"

---

[11] As one lepidopterist has noted, "in the fabric of nature, no thread follows so simple a path as 'either/or'." Jo Brewer, *Butterflies* (New York: Harry N. Abrams, Inc., 1976), p. 104.

[12] For an application, see Walter C. Clemens, Jr., "Soviet Policy toward Europe," in Roman Kolkowicz et al., *The Soviet Union and Arms Control: A Superpower Dilemma* (Baltimore: Johns Hopkins University Press, 1970), pp. 149–80.

[13] For further discussion, see Walter C. Clemens, Jr., *The Superpowers and Arms Control: From Cold War to Interdependence* (Lexington, Mass.: Lexington Books, 1973), Appendixes A and B, pp. 129–34. For a major effort to confront such problems, see H. Gordon Skilling and Franklyn Griffiths, eds., *Interest Groups in Soviet Politics* (Princeton, N.J.: Princeton University Press, 1973).

[14] See, for example, Brezhnev in *Pravda*, October 12, 1974, p. 2, and Kosygin, *Pravda*, November 3, 1974, p. 2, and discussion in Marshall I. Goldman, "Soviet Raw Materials: Production and Exports," mimeographed (Cambridge, Mass.: Harvard University Russian Research Center, 1976), pp. 19–20.

with the West, and Mikhail Suslov's rather neutral allusions to the new policy emphasizing increased trade and technical ties with the West.[15] The more common practice is for supporters of a deviant position to express themselves indirectly. Sometimes this is done by way of emphasis. Thus, opponents of détente will accent the continued dangers posed by Western imperialism, while proponents emphasize restraints which the growth of the socialist camp imposes on the West.[16] Coded phrases are also used: thus, "problems no country can solve by itself no matter how strong" can introduce an argument in favor either of détente and trade (the Brezhnev official line) *or*, alternatively, a somewhat deviant line emphasizing global interdependence.

Thus, a small divergence in a Soviet statement from the standard line could well mean a more serious disagreement than exists among Western policy makers airing their discords openly. The difficulty in ascertaining the extent of such disagreements is heightened by the tendency among all schools in the Party-government establishment to adorn their views in Marxist-Leninist phraseology (a common practice among many dissidents and even some oppositionists as well).[17]

Soviet Priorities and the Role of Eastern Europe

At least since the death of Stalin, Soviet foreign policy appears to have pursued a hierarchy of objectives: (1) to legitimize the regime of the Communist Party in the Soviet Union (CPSU) and its ideology; (2) to maintain the security of the Soviet state; (3) to uphold and strengthen Soviet influence in Eastern Europe and Outer Mongolia; (4) to promote industrialization of the Soviet economy and gradual improvement in Soviet living standards; and (5) to maintain and strengthen Soviet influence in the international Communist move-

[15] See Bruce B. Parrott, "Technological Progress and Soviet Politics," in John R. Thomas and Ursula M. Kruse-Vaucienne, eds., *Soviet Science and Technology* (Washington, D.C.: George Washington University for the National Science Foundation, 1977), pp. 305–23 at p. 318. Parrott's preliminary survey of speeches by prominent members of the Politburo since 1972 "shows no evidence of overt opposition to the change backed by Brezhnev" (p. 318).

[16] See Walter C. Clemens, Jr., "The Soviet Military and SALT" (Paper delivered at the Conference on the Role of the Military in Communist Societies, Maxwell Air Force Base, November 21, 1975).

[17] On the distinction between dissidents and oppositionists, see Vladimir Brovkin, "The Changing Dimensions of Dissent in the USSR (1965–1975)," M.A. thesis, Georgetown University, Washington, D.C., 1977.

ment and the Third World (a less tangible and less important goal than the first four).

Lesser objectives, such as strengthening Soviet armed forces, may become ends in themselves, but they are also instruments by which to achieve the more important and enduring priorities, such as deterring external attack and supporting Soviet interests in Eastern Europe and elsewhere.[18]

No single quotation from the Soviet press will prove (or disprove) this presumed hierarchy of goals, but Brezhnev's words on November 2, 1977, on the occasion of the sixtieth anniversary of the Bolshevik Revolution expressed the basic sentiments suggested here. He boasted:

> Never before has our country had such a huge economic, scientific and technical potential. Never before has its defense capability been so sound and dependable. Never before have we had such favorable possibilities for carrying out the tasks for which, in the long run, the revolution was accomplished —for the welfare of the masses, unfolding socialist democracy and the harmonious development of the individual.

He affirmed also that "the socialist countries are staunch and reliable friends" of developing countries, particularly those "of socialist orientation." The Soviet Union stands ready, he said, to "support their development along the progressive path," with moral and material backing "including assistance in strengthening their defenses." As for U.S.-Soviet relations, he stressed that "life itself requires that considerations of a long-term character, prompted by a concern for peace, be decisive. . . . There is no lack of will on our part to continue our initiative in developing relations with the United States on the basis of equality and mutual respect."[19]

Though Soviet actions since 1953 seem to have accorded with this ordering, the fact is that Kremlin leaders can and have disagreed on how much attention to give to any of these objectives at a particular time and place. It is not clear whether differences within the Soviet establishment are qualitative or quantitative, a matter of kind or of degree. Probably all Kremlin leaders accept the hierarchy of foreign policy goals outlined above. They disagree on the utility of pursuing certain lesser goals and on the likelihood of attaining them, without jeopardizing other, more important objectives. They disagree

---

[18] See Clemens, *The Superpowers and Arms Control*, pp. 4–8.

[19] Translated in *Soviet World Outlook*, vol. 2, no. 11 (November 15, 1977), pp. 2–3.

also on what methods are likely to bring what results at particular moments in time.

I would argue that the tendencies or schools identified here are real; that they reflect strong personal opinions and values, often reflecting institutional needs (for example, those of the military-industrial complex, as against those charged with improving overall economic performance as well as preserving state security); that coalitions have formed within Soviet society committed to promoting one or another of these policy orientations; and that top leaders such as Khrushchev and, later, Brezhnev, having committed their regimes to the feasibility and desirability of working out major accommodations with the West, can withdraw from such commitments only at great risk to their own prestige and power. Though proponents of the other tendencies (which reflect deviant emphases of the official centrist line) are not so locked in by public statements as are the top centrist leaders, they too feel pressure from other members of their coalitions and institutional affiliations to be unwavering in devotion to the cause.

There exist forces giving structure to Soviet policy making, regardless of whether the general secretary sneezes, is fatigued, or is replaced. Individuals—with their moods and modes of operation—determine particular decisions and can thus be supremely important at critical junctures and at crises; but objective forces and structures reduce the range of options likely to be considered and adopted by Soviet (or American or any other) leaders. Indeed, Peking analysts are probably correct that the Brezhnev-Kosygin regime has essentially carried on Khrushchevism without Khrushchev, even though personal styles of decision making have differed enormously. Apart from Molotov, no top Soviet leader since Stalin has favored a continuation of Stalinism (though several contenders for power may have). This phenomenon is probably the result of the enduring pattern of problems and opportunities presented by the policy-making environment, at home and abroad, considered by men with similar scales of values and background preparation. (Most contenders for power in the Soviet Union in recent decades have had far more homogeneous backgrounds than Missouri haberdasher-judge Truman, patricians Roosevelt and Kennedy, Texas teacher Johnson, General Eisenhower and his vice-president, and farmer-engineer Carter. Soviet foreign ministers Molotov, Shepilov, and Gromyko had more in common than George Marshall, Henry Kissinger, and the corporation lawyers who have served as secretaries of state; U.S. secretaries of defense have been even more heterogeneous than their Soviet counterparts, ranging from corporation managers to whiz kids to a congressman.)

One objective restraint on Soviet policy is the atomic bomb, which, as the CPSU Central Committee informed Peking on July 14, 1963, "does not respect the class principle." A second major restraint is the central place of Eastern Europe in Kremlin thinking about security—internal as well as external. Not only is Eastern Europe conceived as a glacis protecting the U.S.S.R. from Western attack, but it is also seen as a potential incubus or conduit for bourgeois ideological penetration of the socialist fatherland. For both reasons (and for others as well), virtually all Soviet spokesmen, even those with autarkist leanings, insist that maintenance of Soviet controls and institutions of the Soviet type in Eastern Europe and Outer Mongolia is a sine qua non for development of relationships outside the socialist commonwealth.

The CPSU and the fraternal regimes in neighboring countries depend upon each other to sustain their common claim that communism, as pioneered by Lenin, is the wave of the future justifying all hardships. If the Communist Party in any of these countries were compelled to relinquish or share power with other parties, the legitimacy of Communist rule elsewhere would also be questioned. Three decades have deepened the economic dependencies among members of the Council for Mutual Economic Assistance (CEMA), though these relationships remain quite asymmetrical. In the event of an East-West war, these nations would also find themselves militarily dependent upon each other—also asymmetrically.[20]

The most critical asymmetry, however, is that factors strengthening a Communist regime in Eastern Europe (Dubček's liberalism or Ceauşescu's nationalism, for example) may be seen in Moscow as threatening to Soviet objectives. A contradiction then develops between local and Kremlin interests, the latter referred to euphemistically as "interests of the socialist commonwealth."

Moscow knows that—even where allies are generally interdependent—some are more dependent than others, some more satisfied than others. Interdependence can mean different rewards. This helps to explain why some members of the alliance are more papist than the pope—East Germany in 1968, for example—while others often inquire: How many divisions does the pope have, and is he willing to use them against us in this instance? Those regimes that have

---

[20] All these views are implicit in the January 31, 1977, decree of the Central Committee of the CPSU, "On the 60th Anniversary of the October Socialist Revolution." See *Kommunist*, no. 2 (January 1977), pp. 3–18, especially pp. 10–11.

been overeager perceived great value from their relationship with the Soviet-led alliance, while others have focused on its liabilities for them.[21] In short, members of CEMA and the Warsaw Pact know well that there may be conflicts between their common cause domestically and in foreign relations and that economic interests may conflict with political, military, and other goals.[22]

Attempting to smooth over such problems and minimize dislocations in Eastern Europe, the U.S.S.R. has been heavily subsidizing the ailing political economies of Husák's Czechoslovakia and Gierek's Poland and has kept increases in the price of Soviet oil for CEMA nations below the levels set by the Organization of Petroleum Exporting Countries (OPEC).

Although Soviet claims for the "socialist commonwealth" as a new model for international relations based on mutually advantageous collaboration may be traced to the 1950s, the "world socialist system" has been praised in ever stronger terms in the 1970s.[23] Recalling Marx's positive views of "mutual dependence" between peoples, a 1975 Soviet article affirms that the fraternal socialist countries practice "mutual aid" rooted in the "organic interconnectedness" of proletarian internationalism with "common democratic principles—equality, respect for sovereignty and national independence and mutually advantageous cooperation."[24] "Socialist economic integration," according

---

[21] Brezhnev told the Twenty-fifth Congress of the CPSU that, as each socialist nation flourishes, its sovereignty is strengthened and the basis for greater commonality in their mutual relations heightened—in politics, in economics, and in social life. Gradually, Brezhnev added, there is a leveling out in development. But he modified this deterministic picture by stating that the pace and level of these trends depend on the degree to which the ruling parties overcome closed-mindedness (*zamknutosti*) and national particularity. Report delivered February 24, 1976, in *Materialy XXV s"ezda KPSS* (Moscow: Politizdat, 1976), pp. 3–89 at p. 6. See also ongoing research by Ronald H. Linden of the University of Pittsburgh.

[22] As one Soviet commentator put it, one cannot automatically transfer the "laws of national economics to the world of socialist economics." *Mirovaia ekonomika i mezhdunarodnye otnosheniia* (hereinafter cited as *MEMO*), no. 6 (June 1976), p. 132.

[23] As for China, Soviet spokesmen continue to affirm that there are no "antagonistic contradictions" between the Chinese people and those of the Soviet Union and other socialist countries. Rather, there is a coincidence of long-term interests. But there are contradictions between the leadership of the Chinese Communist Party (CCP) and Chinese people, and between the CCP ideology and Marxist-Leninist ideology. (See *MEMO*, no. 6 [June 1976], p. 134.) While Moscow still perceives contradictions between socialist and capitalist states, it leans more toward accommodation with the West than with Peking. (See *Materialy XXV s"ezda KPSS*, pp. 10–11.)

[24] I. Dudinskii, "Mirovaia sotsialisticheskaia sistema—novaia mezhdunarodnaia istoricheskaia obshchnost'," *MEMO*, no. 10 (October 1975), pp. 14–16.

to a 1975 Soviet book on CEMA, is a "new category in the political economy of socialism" and the "chief regularity in the development of the world socialist economy." The "international socialist division of labor" is another blessing of CEMA, as manifested, for example, in the coal industry of Eastern Europe.[25] This principle is the ideal, to which the international division of labor among other states—capitalist-capitalist, capitalist-socialist, developing-socialist, and so on—can be at best an imperfect approximation. Mutual complementarity [*vzaimodopolniaemost'*] of CEMA economies has been assured in the long-range Complex Program of Socialist Economic Integration adopted in 1971. In the first five years of the program, Soviet Prime Minister Aleksei Kosygin reported in 1976, the CEMA countries achieved more progress toward economic and scientific-technical cooperation than in the preceding decade.[26]

Moscow's deep and abiding concern with Eastern Europe was reflected in Brezhnev's report to the 1976 Congress of the CPSU in which he affirmed that, though the Politburo must now weigh developments in the remotest corners of the world, the area closest "to our mind and heart" is where Communist ideals are being implemented. Not a single meeting of the Politburo takes place, said Brezhnev, without discussion of ways to increase the unity and the strength of the fraternal socialist countries and to work out common international positions. The socialist camp is growing ever stronger—a gain for all who value freedom, equality, independence, peace, and progress—while its "gradual drawing together [*sblizhenie*] now operates as an objective law [*zakonomernost'*]."[27]

---

[25] V. P. Sergeev and F. N. Sherviakov, *Ekonomicheskaia integratsiia i sovershenstvovanie mekhanizma sotrudnichestva stran-chlenov SEV* (Moscow: Mysl', 1975), p. 8 and chap. 6. Lest any observers pay heed to the critics of CEMA in the West or Peking, let them read a rebuttal to such fabrications and falsifications: O. B. Labetskii, ed., *Sotsialisticheskie mezhdunarodnye otnosheniia i ikh kritiki* (Moscow: Mezhdunarodnye otnosheniia, 1975).

[26] See L. Nikolaev and A. Sokolov, "Novyi vklad v razvitie sotsialisticheskogo sodruzhestva," *MEMO*, no. 9 (September 1976), pp. 15–23 at p. 16.

[27] Brezhnev included in this discussion not only the member nations of CEMA, including Outer Mongolia and Cuba, but also Yugoslavia, Vietnam, and Democratic Korea. He extended greetings also to the patriots of Laos and Cambodia. *Materialy XXV s"ezda KPSS*, pp. 5–6ff.

2
Competing Tendencies

I was impressed against my will by the ability of the Russian to adapt to the customs of those peoples among whom he happens to live; I don't know whether this quality of mind warrants reproach or praise, only that it shows incredibly the Russian's flexibility and the presence of that clear common sense which forgives evil wherever it seems necessary or impossible to destroy.

M. Iu. Lermontov, 1954

Détente should be universal and all-embracing. In our time when technology, including military technology, is developing so rapidly, when the interconnection between the various areas of the world is becoming ever closer, any local conflict can easily develop into a general one. . . .

I shall emphasize another thing: the Soviet Union, just as the other countries of socialism, naturally does not bear responsibility either for the consequences of colonialism or for the baneful influence that the remaining inequality in economic relations has on the developing countries.

Leonid Brezhnev, 1977

Détente and Trade

All Soviet spokesmen agree on the need to perfect collaboration within CEMA and the Warsaw Pact, but some analysts and Kremlin leaders advocate extending ties with the world beyond or, at least, certain sections of it. Though such contacts entail risks, the overall benefits to the Soviet Union are expected to outweigh the likely losses. Those who favor heightened contacts disagree whether Soviet policy should cultivate relations with the United States, Western Europe, Japan, or certain parts of the Third World. They disagree also over the importance to be assigned to political and strategic ties on the one hand, and to economic, technological, or environmental associations on the other.

M. Iu. Lermontov, *Geroi nashevo vremeni* [Hero of our Time] (Kiev: Goslitizdat Ukrainy, 1954), words of the auditor of Maksim Maksimovich, p. 23, translation by Walter C. Clemens, Jr.; Brezhnev, answers to questions posed by *Le Monde* and published in *Izvestiia*, June 16, 1977.

The major concerns of the centrist faction dominating the making of most Soviet foreign policy since Stalin's death have been the need to cultivate détente and trade with the West. Beginning with Malenkov's assertion in 1954 that nuclear war would be catastrophic for all mankind, Soviet leaders have tended to recognize that modern weapons have made their country and the other nuclear powers dependent upon one another for survival. Though some Soviet leaders (like some Americans) continue to suggest ways that one or the other superpower might prevail, Moscow has generally assumed that the destinies of the Soviet Union and the West depend on mutual avoidance of nuclear war.

Soviet recognition of strategic vulnerability is probably the primordial force behind the Kremlin's drive for closer business relations with the West and for arms controls that would reduce defense expenditures. Moscow's interests in trade between East and West and arms limitation reflect the weaknesses of the Soviet economy and are weighty in themselves, but the deepest motive may well be the hope of the leaders that commercial ties and security agreements will improve the prospects for peace. The Marxist materialist bias in Kremlin peace policy is evidenced, for example, in recurrent affirmations by Brezhnev and Soviet scholars that international economic cooperation is an "effective material support" for peaceful relations among states.

Acceptance of mutual strategic interdependence is accompanied by many contradictory streams of behavior: (1) Moscow welcomes official recognition by the United States that SALT and other arms controls should be based on "equal security." (2) Soviet spokesmen stress that the West's acceptance of détente and diminished will to intervene in the Third World are the result of changes in the correlation of forces favoring the socialist camp. (3) But Soviet strategists argue that the West continues to lead in many domains of military power and therefore has no right to demand asymmetrical reductions in Soviet forces in Europe or elsewhere. (4) Moscow spares its reading public the details of SALT I or the Vladivostok agreements, apparently to keep its own people from knowing the realities of the balance of power.

What factors have conditioned this outlook? First, the Soviet leaders have become increasingly confident since the mid-1950s that, for the first time in Russian history, their country possesses the means to deter attack by any rational outside force. At the same time, the Politburo has come to accept the sober reality that it cannot prevent a determined attacker from inflicting horrendous casualties upon

Soviet society and industry and has therefore agreed to forgo large-scale antimissile defenses.

A rounded understanding of U.S.-Soviet relations would take note of the ways in which the arsenals of each superpower have been developed partly in response to moves by the other side. Many Western scholars have stressed the extent to which the United States and other NATO governments have helped bring about the Cold War and arms race. No official Soviet commentaries have acknowledged that the U.S.S.R. may have helped fuel these rivalries.[1] Indeed, during most of the 1960s Soviet spokesmen would not concede that a Russian antiballistic missile system might lead the United States to step up her offensive arms. A major article by Georgii Arbatov in *Pravda* (February 5, 1977) asserted that the U.S.S.R. was only trying to catch up—not surpass—the United States in strategic arms. Similarly, Brezhnev's November 2, 1977, speech reiterated that the U.S.S.R. was not seeking military superiority: "We do not want to upset the approximate equilibrium of military strength existing at present. . . . But in exchange we insist that no one else should seek to upset it in his favor." Brezhnev noted that "new modifications and types of weapons of mass destruction are being developed and it is well known on whose initiative this is being done." He avoided mentioning any new system Moscow might be developing. Until Soviet spokesmen recognize how much Soviet words and deeds fan Western anxieties, Russian audiences will have a less than complete picture of strategic interdependence. Even more important, Moscow will be less likely to exercise the self-restraint which both sides must practice if the arms race is to be curtailed.

The U.S.S.R. has contributed little to international efforts to contain terrorism in other countries, but has chosen instead to gain whatever political benefits might be derived from extending a tacit or open approval to such actions *abroad*. This approach could well become counterproductive, for it sacrifices important security goals for will-o'-the-wisp affections of radical movements. Events of the mid-1970s also suggest that the U.S.S.R. is again becoming vulnerable to domestic terrorism.

A broad view of U.S.-Soviet strategic problems would also take account of the vulnerability of each country to nuclear and other

---

[1] N. S. Khrushchev has acknowledged, however, that the February 1948 "assumption of power by the working class" in Czechoslovakia "increased tensions with our former allies. I would even say England, France, and the United States were frightened by what happened in Czechoslovakia." See Walter C. Clemens, Jr., "*Kto Kovo?* The Present Danger, as Seen from Moscow," *Worldview*, vol. 20, no. 9 (September 1977), pp. 4–9 at p. 8.

attacks by third parties. In 1967–1968, Moscow and Washington combined forces to obtain wide support for their joint draft of a treaty aimed at halting nuclear spread. The intensity and mutuality of this effort diminished in the early 1970s. Although Soviet strategists have joined Americans in lamenting India's capacity to test and develop nuclear weapons, Moscow has remained silent for the most part while Washington takes the heat from open pressure aimed at keeping India, Brazil, Pakistan, South Korea, and others from acquiring independent capacities for nuclear weapons. Though the Kremlin has often sided with the United States in the London meetings of Nuclear Suppliers Group (established 1975), Moscow's reluctance to join the United States openly in strong antiproliferation efforts has weakened prospects of plugging the dike against a flood of plutonium and other nuclear dangers. In August 1977, however, a Soviet initiative, strongly backed by Washington and Paris, apparently led South Africa to forswear plans for an atomic explosion.[2] In late 1977 and early 1978 there was new movement toward improved collaboration and tighter export controls by nuclear fuel suppliers in Western Europe, North America, and the Soviet Union.

What have been the political and military considerations behind the Kremlin's approach to strategic interdependence? First, Soviet leaders from Khrushchev through Brezhnev and Kosygin have staked their careers on the feasibility of achieving far-reaching accommodations with the United States and other Western nations.

Second, Moscow has assumed that East-West commerce would generate material guarantees of peaceful coexistence which would also benefit the Soviet economy. The Kremlin expects that Soviet economic development will be aided by injections of Western technology, credit, and grain. But Russia's economic well-being is not expected to become seriously vulnerable to zigs and zags in Western economic behavior. The Soviet economy may be sensitive (as reflected in higher prices of Western goods passed on to Soviet buyers in the wake of serious inflation in the West), but hardly vulnerable in the way that Japan is vulnerable because of its dependence upon foreign oil. The rate and character of Soviet economic development can be promoted by beneficial ties with the West, even though the overall thrust of material progress in the Soviet Union is self-sustaining.

Moscow probably expects that Western economic life will be-

[2] On the Nuclear Suppliers Group, see Takashi Oka, "Soviets, U.S. Strange Allies on World Nuclear Limits," *Christian Science Monitor*, June 15, 1977, p. 26; on the South African affair, see a front-page story in the *Washington Post*, August 28, 1977.

come more dependent upon East-West trade than upon the Soviet Union or its CEMA allies. If a firm such as Fiat or a country such as Italy comes to count on large deals with the U.S.S.R., it will become more sensitive—perhaps even vulnerable—to the strings manipulated by the supercorporation known as the Soviet Union. Moscow may be able to influence even the government of the United States through the intermediary of the Chase Manhattan Bank or the many other firms (and farms) looking for profits in the vast Soviet market.

In a world in which all countries become increasingly dependent upon external sources of supply and markets, the U.S.S.R. is probably the least vulnerable of industrial states. The Kremlin would like foreign technology to tap the resources of Siberia; it would like turnkey plants and blueprints to facilitate modernization of its own economy; it would like assured supplies of Western grain to change the ratio of protein to carbohydrates in Soviet diets. But Russia could also do without such transactions; they might facilitate modernization and help improve economic growth, but none is essential to the survival of the Soviet state or, probably, of the CPSU regime. Though the U.S.S.R. also depends on external sources for some minerals, such as bauxite, the list of critical materials that must be imported is much shorter for Russia than for the United States, and the volume is much less.[3] Some major imports come from Eastern Europe or the People's Republic of China.[4] The major question on the resource horizon is probably petroleum, which Russia may need to import by the mid-1980s.[5]

The CIA estimates that Soviet GNP will grow at an annual rate of 3 to 4 percent from the late 1970s to the mid-1980s and that per capita consumption will grow at no more than 2 percent a year, in contrast to about 3.5 percent from 1965 through 1977.[6] A variety of problems limit the Kremlin's ability to alter this picture—the drying up of rural sources of growth in the urban labor force, a slowdown

---

[3] See Theodore Shabad, "Raw Material Problems of the Soviet Aluminum Industry" (pp. 661–76), and related essays in *Soviet Economy in a New Perspective,* A Compendium of Papers Presented to the Joint Economic Committee, U.S. Congress (Washington, D.C., October 14, 1976).

[4] See the statement by General George S. Brown to the Congress on the Defense Posture of the United States for fiscal 1978, prepared January 20, 1977, p. 103.

[5] CIA study released by the White House in April 1977. The CIA estimate might be altered if the Soviet Union could use more natural gas where oil is now being used. Such conversions, in turn, depend partially on access to Western technology.

[6] See U.S. Congress Subcommittee on Priorities and Economy in Government of the Joint Economic Committee, *Soviet Economic Problems and Prospects* (Washington, D.C., 1977), pp. ix–x. If the Soviet leaders proceed on the basis of business as usual, GNP growth may drop to 2 percent a year between 1985 and 1990. Ibid., p. 18.

in growth of capital productivity, an inefficient agricultural system combined with a likely return of the more normal but harsher climatic patterns that prevailed in the 1960s, a limited capacity to earn hard currency abroad to pay for imports, and, finally, a reluctance or inability to convert defense capacity to civilian uses.

What may be the impact of imported Western technology? It will probably be important in helping the Soviet chemical industry and extraction of oil and gas, but funds to purchase equipment for these industries are likely to shrink if Soviet oil exports decline. Overall, imports from the West have accounted for only 5 percent of total Soviet investment in machinery and equipment from 1972 to 1977. So far there has been little wider benefit or demonstrable effect on Soviet productivity beyond the immediate point of application. The slowness of assimilation and diffusion of foreign technology have been widely noted in the U.S.S.R., and a number of decrees have endeavored to improve performance, but it "seems unreasonable to count on a breakthrough over the next several years."[7]

The greatest limitation on Moscow's willingness to expand its ties with the West probably comes from the perennial Kremlin concern to maintain rigid political controls at home and in Eastern Europe. From the Lacy-Zarubin agreement of 1958 through the Helsinki Declaration of 1975, the Soviet leaders have assumed that the Soviet Union could successfully contain any erosive effects from détente and associations with the West upon the foundations of Party power. A content analysis of party journals such as *Kommunist* and *Partiinaia zhizn'* from 1965 through the mid-1970s found little concern, at least before 1977, that détente might poison Soviet minds and undermine the allegiance of the population, but this may be because the regime assumed that the task of preserving ideological purity could be left to the highest party organs and the KGB.[8] The record also shows

---

[7] Ibid., p. 13.

[8] Both publications in the 1970s paid their respects to the "peace programme" of the CPSU, and to the work of General Secretary Brezhnev in promoting and implementing it. *Kommunist* also published many articles admitting the complexity and interconnectedness of contemporary world problems; *Partiinaia zhizn'*, in contrast, practically reveled in parochialism: In 1975 about 50 percent of its articles were devoted to organizational problems important to municipal and regional leaders of the party, with virtually no reference to ways in which comparable problems are handled in other countries; about 30 percent of the articles dealt with propaganda and ideology, basically from an agitational perspective; about 15 percent of the articles discussed the role of the party in industrial and agricultural enterprises, with no mention of the ties between the Soviet economy and the outside world; perhaps 5 percent of the articles concerned foreign policy matters—for example, the victory over German capitalists and "landowners" (*pomeshchiki*) in World War II or the relationships of Europe's "peasants" (*sic*) to the EEC.

that the Kremlin has overestimated the stability of its rule, especially in Eastern Europe, where anti-Soviet challenges emerged in 1953, 1956, 1968, 1970–1971, and 1975–1977.

While these challenges were more open and better organized in Eastern Europe, they reverberated within the U.S.S.R., helping to generate a dissident movement that has echoed in many segments of Soviet society, seeming to confirm the darkest fears of some autarkists. In response to criticisms of Soviet human rights policies by the Carter administration in 1977, however, Moscow staged a broad counterattack. *Kommunist,* for example, explained the ideological attack by the West as the attempt of a dying way of life to delay its inevitable defeat in the historic rivalry with a new world. Countering the increasingly sophisticated appeals of bourgeois propagandists would give the U.S.S.R. an enhanced opportunity to carry the ideas of Marxism-Leninism to all mankind.[9]

Globalism

"The division of mankind threatens it with destruction," Andrei D. Sakharov wrote in his 1968 manifesto. "Only universal cooperation . . . will preserve civilization."

Writing still within a Marxist framework, Sakharov praised the "lofty moral ideals of socialism and labor," but he also condemned "bureaucratized dogmatism" and called for systematic collaboration between East and West to prevent war and overcome poverty. Going beyond official Soviet concerns at the time, he also called for action to halt the population explosion and cope with world hunger. Contending that environmental pollution was by no means confined to the capitalist world, Sakharov warned that the "problem of geohygiene" could "not be solved on a national and especially not on a local basis." His greatest challenge to the CPSU regime, however, was his argument that "intellectual freedom is essential" for a "scientific democratic approach to politics, economy, and culture."[10]

The most important institutional support for globalism in the U.S.S.R. establishment has come from the State Committee on Science and Technology, established in 1965 and given sizable budgetary resources in recent years to promote the application of science and technology to economic development (leaving the Academy of Sci-

---

[9] See L. Tolkunov, "U perednego kraia ideologicheskoi bor"by," *Kommunist,* no. 2 (January 1977), pp. 116–25.

[10] Andrei D. Sakharov, *Progress, Coexistence and Intellectual Freedom* (New York: W. W. Norton, 1968), pp. 27–30, 49.

ences to emphasize fundamental science).[11] On July 8, 1972, as the details of the U.S.-Soviet science and technology agreement were being negotiated, the deputy chairman of the committee, Dzhermen M. Gvishiani, wrote in *Pravda* that commercial and technological expediency were pushing farsighted representatives of U.S. industry, science, and technology toward contacts with the U.S.S.R. They were seen as overpowering those conservative circles which sought to hold back contacts and trade through tariff barriers and export controls.

The chairman of the state committee, V. A. Kirillin, has stressed in articles, speeches, and interviews since 1972 that no country could effectively cover all of science and technology and that there ought to be a division of labor. The U.S.S.R. had decided not to try to go it alone and wished to develop science and technology jointly with other countries.[12]

Though Sakharov's appeals to the Kremlin met official silence or quiet rebuffs, the essence of his 1968 manifesto has been incorporated into an important strain of official Soviet thinking: that there is now a "globalism of problems." As late as 1972, the U.S.S.R. bypassed the United Nations Environmental Conference in Stockholm because East Germany would not be represented. And most Soviet spokesmen have rejected the limits-to-growth arguments current in the West since the early 1970s. But beginning around 1971 a number of Soviet publications gave increasing attention to global problems—environmental, political, economic, and others.[13]

The complexity of such problems was fully conceded by a number of scholars drawn from many fields to contribute to a symposium sponsored by the journal *Problems of Philosophy* and reported in *Literaturnaia gazeta* on January 24, 1973.[14] Several academicians re-

---

[11] Loren Graham, "The Place of the Academy of Sciences System in the Overall Organization of Soviet Science," in Thomas and Kruse-Vaucienne, *Soviet Science and Technology*, pp. 44–62 at pp. 45–46.

[12] See Loren Graham, "Speculative Analysis of the Soviet Perception of the S&T Agreement," in *Review of the US/USSR Agreement on Cooperation in the Fields of Science and Technology* (Washington, D.C.: Board on International Scientific Exchange, Commission on International Relations, National Academy of Sciences, May 1977), pp. 62–79 at pp. 74–75.

[13] For a study of how industrial groups and their local party allies have been able to thwart high-level decrees since 1969 (provoked in part by environmental protection lobbies) aimed at improving the water quality of Lake Baikal, see Donald R. Kelley, "Environmental Policy-Making in the USSR: The Role of Industrial and Environmental Interest Groups," *Soviet Studies*, vol. 28, no. 4 (October 1976), pp. 570–89. Kelley's article also contains many valuable bibliographical citations. *Literaturnaia gazeta* and *Komsomolskaia pravda* seem to have been in the forefront of the Soviet ecological movement.

[14] "Global Ecology: A New Science," *Literaturnaia gazeta*, January 24, 1973, p. 12.

called the role of their late colleague Vladimir I. Vernadskii, who, before World War II, helped to create a holistic vision of man and his habitat. Taking the concept of the noosphere from Teilhard de Chardin, Vernadskii gave it a new and different meaning: Rather than a layer of thought, over and above nature, Vernadskii saw the noosphere as a stratum of thought and work—immanent in the biosphere rather than above or beyond it, with man becoming the most powerful geological force.[15]

Is the biosphere in danger? Yes, was the most frequent answer of the scientists and philosophers assembled, though they added that a crisis could be averted. Despite some bows to official optimism, *Literaturnaia gazeta* left its readers with an impression of the difficulties in the man-nature-technology equation rather than the facility with which they could be resolved. All participants stressed that the equation could be solved only by admitting that its ramifications were global and complex and by unifying or integrating many branches of science.

While the *Literaturnaia gazeta* report was focused on ecological problems, global issues of a political nature were emphasized by V. Osipov writing in *Izvestiia* the following month.[16] "The logic of coexistence," he declared, "emerges from a whole series of new factors in the life of the international community of states which until recently either did not exist or did not have the significance which they are acquiring in the last ten to fifteen years." No longer can there be purely "local" wars, for conflicts such as Vietnam and the Middle East threaten all nations. Thus, the Clausewitz dictum that war is an extension of politics can no longer be valid (though it once was—a bow to Lenin). Western countries are faced with severe fuel and mineral resource shortages (this was written before the 1973 oil embargo). United Nations studies point to environmental problems threatening to engulf mankind. Thus, "not one of these problems can be solved by individual states no matter how strong or rich they may be. To cope with them, joint efforts of many, many countries are needed and, consequently, collaboration among them, for no other approach is feasible today." The globalism of problems dictates that farsighted, responsible leaders consider not only what divides their countries but also how they can help and complement each other.

---

[15] Vernadskii published his book *The Biosphere* in Leningrad in 1926. See Kendall E. Bailes, "Ecology and History in the USSR: Vernadsky and the Biosphere," unpublished manuscript, University of California, Irvine, 1977.

[16] V. Osipov, "The Logic of Coexistence," *Izvestiia*, February 17, 1973. By coincidence, one of the leading dissident isolationists (referred to below) is named V. N. Osipov.

Capitalism, of course, has not changed its essence, and only time will tell whether the Western governments will face up to the new realities. Meanwhile, the logic of coexistence calls for détente and for "all-round, fruitful and mutually advantageous collaboration among all states regardless of their social structure."

A similar view was presented to a U.S. industrial conference in September 1973 by the deputy chairman of the Council of Ministers State Committee on Science and Technology. Dzhermen M. Gvishiani contended that

> the difference in social systems does not exclude the existence of the needs and interests common to both systems. All of us, living on this planet, are contemporaries and co-inhabitants. The world history in the past was the history of separate regions more or less independent of each other. At present we speak of the history of humanity as a whole despite all social, political, racial or other differences. *The interdependence of nations and continents is an obvious fact from which one cannot escape.* In this respect, the entire humanity has a common fate. All of us, if one may say so, are aboard the same spaceship which, by the way, does not have any exhaust pipes. (Emphasis added.)

Gvishiani argued that

> humanity is able to improve and multiply natural conditions of its life. But for that one needs new social orientations, a new understanding of the richness of society which must not be evaluated one-sidedly, judged solely in monetary terms.[17]

While emphasizing the need for constructive contributions by Western business interests to global problems, Gvishiani affirmed that "there are problems, the solution of which presupposes international cooperation, concerted activities of all nations." "We are decisively opposed to the ideology of isolationism," said Gvishiani, because "there exists the historically formed division of labor which is an objective condition of mutually beneficial cooperation between countries in . . . science, technology, and economy."[18]

---

[17] Address by Dzhermen M. Gvishiani at the International Industrial Conference jointly sponsored by the Conference Board and Stanford Research Institute, September 17–21, 1973, San Francisco.

[18] Ibid. The division of labor Dr. Gvishiani refers to is between socialist and capitalist states. In Soviet parlance, it is to be distinguished from the "international socialist division of labor," which exists only among socialist states.

Following a number of positive references to global interdependence in 1973, Soviet spokesmen had much less to say on this subject from late 1973 until late 1976. Why? Had globalism emerged only under the aegis of the 1972–1973 Nixon-Brezhnev summits? Did the uncertainties of the Nixon-Ford transition in 1974 and the fading of détente amid Angola and a U.S. election year dim Moscow's global perspectives? "These factors played a role," a leading Soviet *mezhdunarodnik* told the author in 1977, "but we had our internal problems as well."

While globalism received less explicit support in 1974–1976, functional cooperation with the West in science and in environmental collaboration continued to win approval from the Kremlin. The Soiuz-Apollo space mission in 1975 elicited in *Kommunist* what amounted to an appeal for more Soviet-American functional cooperation in technological domains outside the political sphere. Thus, the chief trainer of Soviet cosmonauts wrote that the Soiuz-Apollo linkup, more than just an experiment with technical systems, was above all a valuable step in the development and broadening of international collaboration in science generally and in space research in particular. V. Shatalov further contended that "the present stage of scientific-technological development progress increasingly places before humanity singularly difficult tasks of a general planetary character." This tendency underlies "the necessity for joining efforts of different countries, among them the U.S.S.R. and U.S.A., to realize multifaceted, complex projects, scientific research and experiments for peaceful purposes." His colleague, B. Petrov, head of Intercosmos (the membership of which corresponds to CEMA), recounted not only Soviet cooperative programs with East European countries but also with India.

Did politics impede the Soiuz-Apollo collaboration? *Kommunist* asked. No, was the reply. Neither political nor linguistic nor technological differences obstructed these efforts. The *New York Daily News* had urged America to back out because it would give much but get little. In reality, both Shatalov and Petrov argued, the Soviet and U.S. programs had developed independently to such a high level that neither was in a position to "acquire something at the expense of the other." Neither could make some kind of "radical breakthrough" just by adopting the other's technical experience, said Shatalov (himself a lieutenant general). Apparently addressing Soviet hard-liners, he declared: "It would be naive to assume that the Americans, learning something from Soviet specialists, let us say, the 'secret' of the composition of a two-gas artificial atmosphere in space ships, would immediately convert their ships from one-gas atmosphere to the two-gas which, as the Americans concede, has many advantages."

The Soiuz-Apollo mission was thus in effect put forward as a paradigm for solving common problems on the basis of parallel evolution rather than "convergence." Such collaboration required "mutual trust, open, honest and friendly relations, a continual readiness to facilitate the success and well-being of one's colleagues." The mastery of outer space, said Petrov, would benefit "all humanity" and remind Soviet citizens that "our country is the native land of *kosmonavtiki*."[19]

In retrospect, however, it appears that the main Soviet aim in the Soiuz-Apollo effort was to clinch in another domain the image of Soviet parity with the United States. There was little exchange of technology except for the docking device. Since 1975 the Soviets have shown no sign of wanting to join the International Telecommunications Satellite Corporation, even though terminals have been set up in the U.S.S.R. (and China). U.S. NASA experts have been allowed to visit one area of the Soviet Union to collect "ground truth" for a project to monitor crops by remote sensing from space vehicles, but Moscow still opposes open dissemination of remote sensing data. Soviet diplomats have joined United Nations majorities opposing space "intrusions" and public release of resulting data, probably for propaganda reasons and because Soviet sensing technology is less advanced than American. Moscow has also joined those countries that oppose direct broadcasting from satellites, claiming that it constitutes external interference in internal affairs of receiving countries. The launching of the thousandth Soviet Kosmos satellite on March 31, 1978, provoked a *Le Monde* analysis (April 4) showing that at least 782 of the vehicles (in a series begun in 1962) have had military missions. Nonetheless, Gherman Titov, the Soviet Union's second man in space in 1961—now a major general in the Air Force—confirmed Moscow's interest in "the possible use of the proposed American space shuttle to carry men and supplies to the Soviet Salyut orbiting stations"—another sign that space collaboration could still be used to deepen East-West interdependence.[20]

One of the most important arenas for functional collaboration between East and West lies in the preservation and enhancement of our common *oikos*—Greek for home or habitat. *Kommunist* carried

---

[19] The heading for both statements was: "Outer Space Serves the Peoples." B. Petrov's was entitled "Orbits of Acquaintanceship [*posnaniia*] and Collaboration"; V. Shatalov's, " 'Soiuz' and 'Apollo' Lay the Road to the 'Cosmic Tomorrow,' " *Kommunist*, no. 10 (July 1975), pp. 76–87.

[20] *Christian Science Monitor*, February 15, 1978, p. 21.

three articles on this subject in November 1975.[21] The first proclaimed the "interdependence" of economic progress and ecological well-being. Quoting Engels, economist M. Lemeshev argued that it is wrong to think about "conquering nature." The use of nature is a "global process" which should be goal-oriented. Technology should be refined, laws strengthened, international cooperation expanded. A second article, on the "ecologization of production," reported research findings on ways to preserve the environment while maintaining or increasing productivity, but it lamented that most conservation groups in the U.S.S.R. were not technically prepared to analyze such problems and, most important, were geared for protection of nature instead of its reproduction. A third essay, on the ideological aspects of ecological problems, called on the Soviet press to give more attention to refuting Western charges that the U.S.S.R. pollutes and destroys its environment as badly as or worse than systems rooted in private ownership. This charge resonates not only in the U.S.S.R. but in the Third World countries that are trying to decide "which route" to follow. The negative impact of capitalism on the environment must be weighed along with "historical heritage, the results of uncoordinated actions by contemporary humanity, and senseless expenditures on armaments." Still, research and cooperation with the West should not be ignored. "Not by accident" the first treaty signed by the Soviet Union and the United States in May 1972 had environmental protection as its aim.[22]

In the pugnacious spirit recommended by party ideologues, world aspects of the ecological crisis were discussed in *International Affairs* in February 1977. Three-fourths of the article exposed the social roots of the crisis, contending that the United States causes half the world's pollution and approving Gus Hall's view that humanity must choose between capitalism and survival. After listing Soviet environmental protection laws adopted since 1969, the article produced a non sequitur:

> Environmental protection is an urgent problem for all states and therefore necessitates international cooperation. Firstly, the environment is indivisible: it is obviously impossible to contain pollution within the borders of one country. Sec-

[21] M. Lemeshev, "Ekonomika i ekologiia: ikh vzaimosviaz' i zavisimost'," *Kommunist*, no. 17 (November 1975), pp. 47–55; A. Nagornyi, O. Siziakin, and K. Skuf'yn, "Nekotorye voprosy ekologizatsii proizvodstva," pp. 56–64; I. Laptev, "Ideologischeskie aspekty ekologicheskikh problem," pp. 65–73.

[22] In fact, the first treaty pledged each side to cooperate in public health and medical science; the second (signed later the same day), in environmental protection.

> ondly, however powerful a country's economic, scientific and technological potential, it cannot solve single-handed all problems. . . . Finally, international specialisation and cooperation . . . would speed up the creation of "wasteless" technologies and pollution control facilities and . . . bring down the expenses while . . . boosting economic returns.[23]

Kremlin ideologists seek to rationalize environmental cooperation with capitalism while portraying the Western countries as the main villains in ecological disruption. The Soviet reader may well be confused. If pollution is not a supraclass problem, why study this problem with the West? If social systems are to blame, why look for a technological fix? If the Soviet system does not exploit man or his environment, why have Russia's rivers and air become so polluted in recent decades (as documented in *Kommunist* and other Soviet publications)? Is this a local or a global problem—or both? If it has global characteristics, what does this say about the convergence thesis?

Scientists such as the biologists collaborating in one of the *Kommunist* articles may be primarily concerned for environmental well-being; economists such as Lemeshev may feel that productivity and environmental preservation go hand in hand; such persons are aware of global interdependence and may favor pragmatic steps at home and abroad, leaving it to party ideologues to rationalize the necessary policies. Defenders of the faith, however, are squeezed from all sides: Brezhnev has come out for détente and environmental cooperation with the West. How can all this be squared with the party's ideological claims?

A thoughtful reader might well conclude that pollution in the U.S.S.R. is not the result of historical factors or capitalism, but the manner in which the U.S.S.R. has industrialized under socialism. He might note too that one of the solutions advocated is the creation of a new generation of pollution-free technology, even though ideologues attack the notion that technology (a supraclass phenomenon) is the villain. (If he talked with members of the Soviet fishing fleet or could observe its wasteful and abusive practices, he might even conclude that the modus operandi of the Soviet economic and bureaucratic system presents a special threat to the global environment.)

Issues of global interdependence emerged again in many Soviet publications in late 1976 and early 1977.[24] The most authoritative

---

[23] G. Chernikov, "The Ecological Crisis: Problems and Solutions," *International Affairs* (Moscow), no. 2 (February 1977), pp. 52–60.

[24] A. Sergiyev, "Bourgeois Theories of 'Interdependence' Serve Neocolonialism," *International Affairs*, no. 11 (November 1976), p. 103–11; A. A. Kokoshin, "Vzaimozavisimost': real'nosti, kontseptsii i politika," *SShA*, no. 1 (January 1977),

comment probably was that of the Party's theoretical organ, *Kommunist.* Global problems, it averred, are a manifestation of a

> qualitatively new stage in the dialectical interaction between man and nature. The scientific-technical revolution, accelerating the development of productive forces, placed in human hands new means for the subjugation of the forces of nature and thereby generated both new interconnections between man and nature and also new conflicts in the course of realizing these interconnections.[25]

Marx and Lenin noted the growth in their times in the sheer "scale of events, intensifying the internationalization of processes and their tendency to become global, that is, encompassing the whole world, all humanity, and each of us in particular."[26]

The reality of global problems is a fact, but it is interpreted divergently in capitalist and socialist societies. Bourgeois reformists in the West equate globalism with "supranationalism," "supraclass," and even supraclass convergence into a "single-industrial society" or "one-world system." Though the present level of science and technology permits resolution of all global problems, they *appear* insoluble in capitalist society because monopoly capital either seeks solutions to

---

pp. 11–22. Kokoshin portrays three schools in the United States: neoisolationism; autarky (similar to but more aggressive than neoisolationism); and interdependence, as exemplified in the writings of Lincoln P. Bloomfield, Zbigniew Brzezinski, and other mainstream analysts. Their concern, according to Kokoshin, is to help Washington make the minimum necessary adjustments to new realities and Third World sensitivities in order to maintain America's hegemonist position.

The weekly *New Times,* for its part, kept up a drumbeat for disarmament and détente but had little to say about extending ties with the world outside CEMA. It reported on the benefits of Intercosmos for East Europe, even though there is no international organization undergirding it, the staff operating in Moscow under the U.S.S.R. Academy of Sciences. The Soviet Union provides space facilities free of charge to the other socialist countries, *New Times* reported, and has recently proposed that their citizens take part in Soviet space missions between 1978 and 1983. The article had nothing to say about Soviet space collaboration outside the CEMA orbit (no. 41 [October 1976], pp. 21–22). Another article (no. 43, pp. 22–23) covered Soviet achievements in forecasting earthquakes, with passing references to useful research in the United States and Japan but only condescension toward China's historical and recent work in seismology. And a report on the Law of the Sea Conference in New York (no. 42, pp. 20–21) was focused on the "non-constructive approach of some states."

On the significance of the joint Soviet-Czechoslovak space flight in March 1978 in Soiuz-28 and on future Intercosmos flights, see articles in *New Times,* no. 11 (March 1978), pp. 4–5, where the reportage smacks more of big brotherly condescension than perceived interdependence in Soviet–East European relations.

[25] V. Zagladin and I. Frolov, "Global'nyie problemy sovremennosti," *Kommunist,* no. 16 (November 1976), pp. 93–104 at p. 101.

[26] Ibid., p. 93.

enhance its egotistical interests or strives to impede solution of global problems.

Western studies such as those by the Club of Rome speak of an "interdependence of crisis situations" affecting the whole world—capitalist and socialist. This is a "false conclusion," because socialist societies know how to deal with such problems and are successfully doing so within CEMA.[27]

An optimal solution to global issues will be possible only when, as Lenin predicted, the proletariat of all nations manages the world economy as a whole. In the meantime, the Communist states set a model for the way of dealing with such issues and demonstrate their willingness to collaborate with capitalist regimes as well.

But divergent understandings of the global problems need not prevent East-West collaboration. Indeed, there is a "dialectical interconnection" between relaxing international tensions and solving global problems. Common efforts on these problems deepen peaceful coexistence because they presuppose intensive economic and scientific-technical collaboration among states with different social systems. Though some self-styled leftists may criticize such collaboration, it enhances the Soviet cause by demonstrating the superiority of socialism.[28]

While some Soviet spokesmen argue the global nature of many contemporary problems, their practical concerns seem to remain détente and trade with the West. It is in East-West relations that the Soviet Union stands to gain (as well as contribute) something substantial. The November 1976 *Kommunist* article, for example, says virtually nothing about global problems in the Third World, but emphasizes the importance of improved East-West relations to cultivate both détente and collaboration in other spheres. While "not departing from the sphere of the sharp struggle of the two systems," world politics today "is built more and more around the positive resolution of certain economic, scientific-technical and cultural tasks, in which contemporary global problems play a highly important role." Resources saved by arms limitations, for example, could be applied to other pressing problems.[29]

In contrast to this situation many Soviet leaders probably fear that Moscow could lose from joint programs in which "northern" nations work together with "southern." They fear charges by ideological opponents in Peking or elsewhere that the Soviet Union has

[27] Ibid., p. 97.
[28] Ibid., pp. 103–104.
[29] Ibid., p. 94.

given up revolution in favor of superpower hegemonism to buttress the status quo, and they fear their comparative disadvantage in working side by side with more technologically advanced nations in the third world. Finally, as noted earlier, the Soviet Union has been less affected by developments in the Third World—economic, ecological, and political—than has the West and has been less attuned to the urgency of truly global collaboration.

Nikolai N. and Margarita Inozemtsev, speaking at the Kennan Institute on May 20, 1977, affirmed that the Soviet Union stands ready to take part in North-South as well as East-West cooperative projects, but had nothing specific to recommend. Another Soviet visitor in 1976 may have been closer to the dominant Kremlin position. A specialist on U.S.-Soviet arms problems, he was asked whether both countries might not need to cooperate with the food and other crises of the less developed nations. His reply: "You feed your allies; we'll feed ours."

Forward Strategy

Another important tendency among the Soviet leaders endorses continued or closer ties with selected Third World nations to attract them to the Soviet camp, to liberate them from capitalist-imperialist influences, and to negate their value to the West as bases, markets, or sources of raw materials. The model for this policy was set in the early 1920s and mid-1930s when Moscow helped the nationalist bourgeoisie of Turkey to resist Western dictation and to struggle for a Black Sea Straits convention more in keeping with the security interests of the Soviet Union.[30]

Moscow's efforts to throttle supplies of vital resources to the West commenced with the Khrushchev-Bulganin campaign to create a more dynamic and influential Soviet presence in the Third World, symbolized by arms sales to Egypt in 1955 and subsequent assistance with the Aswan High Dam.[31] The Soviet Union blessed Arab oil embargoes against the West in 1956, 1967, and 1973, even while continuing to sell Soviet oil and resell Arab oil to Western buyers,

---

[30] For an early account, see *Mezhdunarodnaia politika R.S.F.S.R. v 1922 g.* (Moscow: NKID, 1923), pp. 56–58.

[31] Andrei D. Sakharov recalls a statement by "a highly placed official" in 1955 to a group of Soviet scientists explaining that Soviet diplomacy would henceforth exploit Arab nationalism to create difficulties for the European countries regarding oil supplies. This, Sakharov comments, is the true meaning of Soviet rhetoric about "defending the just cause of the Arab peoples." See his *O strane i mire* (New York: Khronika, 1975), p. 75.

including such prime targets of the 1973 embargo as the Netherlands and the United States.[32] The Kremlin has applauded the formation of cartels of producers not only of oil but of other mineral supplies and raw materials important to OECD countries.

Moscow's forward strategy in the Third World uses a variety of instruments to pursue its objectives, from training programs in the Soviet Union to supplying Soviet pilots in crises.[33] The most enduring constituency for such programs probably comes from those branches of the military, especially portions of the navy, whose claim on allocations expands with growing Soviet involvement in the Third World. Like other warrior classes in the history of imperialism, they have a material stake in expansion for its own sake, regardless of any strict calculation of national gain and loss in such adventures.[34] They find allies in the political elite who, for their own reasons, want a harder line against the West.

Backers of a forward strategy recognize that Communist ideology is far from admired in many Third World nations, and that Soviet assistance has been abused, and Soviet advisers have been expelled by Anwar Sadat and other Third World leaders. But this group contends that the Soviet Union can learn from past mistakes and in time reduce the chances of unnecessary friction with Third World regimes. Meanwhile, Moscow should exploit the dependence of the West upon Third World sources of supply to reduce the economic and military potential of the United States and its allies. If Third World nations become more closely dependent upon CEMA markets, political dependency may be one step behind. Almost any relationship of interdependence between a Third World nation and the Soviet Union will find the smaller partner far more vulnerable than the superpower.

Western talk about North-South interdependence is written off by many Soviet spokesmen as a smoke screen for neoimperialism. Whereas U.S. leaders formerly talked of interdependence to mask their designs for hegemony in Europe, the many economic crises and shortages troubling the West since 1973 have inspired Americans to broaden this slogan to include the Third World (and, in some cases, capitalist-socialist relations as well). While the United States and

---

[32] See Arthur Jay Klinghoffer, *The Soviet Union and International Oil Politics* (New York: Columbia University Press, 1977), chap. 8.

[33] See Walter C. Clemens, Jr., "Soviet Policy in the Third World: Five Alternative Scenarios," in Raymond Duncan, ed., *Soviet Policy in Developing Countries* (Waltham, Mass.: Ginn-Blaisdell, 1970), pp. 313–43.

[34] See Joseph A. Schumpeter, *Imperialism and Social Classes* (New York: World Publishing Company, Meridian Books, 1951).

other Western governments and firms may make some concessions to the Third World in the name of interdependence, the *objective* content of their strategy is counterrevolutionary: It seeks to sustain Western influence and brake the development of Third World nations toward independence and progress. This, at least, is what many Soviet publications contend. They contrast the sham interdependence and unequal relationships spawned by Western imperialists with the genuine interdependence fostered by the U.S.S.R. and other CEMA nations in their associations with the Third World.

Imperialist theories of interdependence with the Third World are portrayed as ideological tools in the same vast arsenal that includes partnership, balance of power, threats, and outright aggression—all aimed at establishing a neocolonial status quo in the former colonies. Thus, Western calls for close economic and political ties with developing countries are accompanied by veiled threats about catastrophes that may result if "unprecedented economic nationalism" prevails over interdependence.[35]

What factors shape Soviet attitudes toward problems of interdependence in the Third World? Many Soviet leaders are less likely to be aware of the organic interdependencies of the world today than are their Western counterparts. First, they have traveled less widely and, when traveling, have been more insulated from deep and informative contacts with local populations. Second, Soviet ideology emphasizes the adequacy of the earth's resources to sustain human needs and tends to write off any shortcomings as results of particular social-economic systems. Thus, for decades Soviet spokesmen have downgraded the need for population controls by contending that, if some Third World nation is starving, the fault must lie in its social and economic system rather than in some limits to growth. Optimistic Marxism rather than pessimistic Malthusianism is further sustained by the fact that the U.S.S.R. has abundant resources, including space, so that more people rather than fewer would be welcome.[36] Since

[35] E. Tarabrin, "'Tretii mir' i imperializm: novoe v sootnoshenii sil," *MEMO*, no. 2 (February 1975), pp. 12–23 at p. 21.

[36] Research being conducted by Helen Desfosses shows that there has been considerable movement from the more dogmatic Soviet positions at the time of the first World Population Conference in 1954 to the 1966 Belgrade Conference and the 1974 Conferences on Population in Bucharest and on Food in Rome. Although in 1974 the Soviets continued to insist that there be no limitations on national sovereignty in the area of demographic policy, they indicated their willingness at Bucharest to accept the need for world population measures. But they also insisted that socialism be recognized as the ultimate solution to the problem of pressure by population on resources. Among the factors accounting for the gradual shifts in Soviet policy, according to Desfosses, are Soviet concern with the food import requirements of the Soviet Union, a fear that population-related

population growth would be desirable for Russia, it must be beneficial for others as well. These blind spots are rigidified still further by an inclination, dating from 1917, to assume that whatever is good for Soviet Russia and its allies is good for the world—a point reiterated by General Secretary Brezhnev at the Twenty-fifth CPSU Congress in 1976.

The Soviet world view tends to see North-South relations in zero-sum terms rather than holistically as vital ingredients in an organically linked world. Instead of *kto komy*—"who will give to whom?" or better, "how can we help each other?"—Moscow still thinks in Leninist terms: *kto kovo*—"who will do in whom?"

Autarky

A fourth tendency, though officially disowned, has significant weight in day-to-day decision making and could become much more important in the future. This is autarky—a school that calls for limiting and, if possible, reducing Soviet vulnerabilities, obligations, and ties to the outside world.

Some autarkists dwell on economic factors, while others are spurred by political or cultural considerations. Some are optimistic about the resources of the Russian people, the Soviet Union, or even the socialist camp as a whole. But others worry about present assets and fear the inroads of external contacts upon the foundations of Soviet power. Officials with autarkist leanings must balance their goals for self-sufficiency against party-line orthodoxies and the practical reasons for expanding ties with the outer world.[37] Only dissidents can call openly for Russia to retire to virginal purity, aloof from the affairs of others.

The most eloquent case for radical autarky is made in Aleksandr

---

instability in the Third World could involve the Soviet Union and endanger détente, the need to come to terms with family planning movements in many countries of the Third World, a desire to counter China's efforts at population control, and an interest in breaking the scientific isolation of Soviet demographers. But there continues to be a series of ideological and political obstacles to changing the longstanding Soviet belief in the ability of science cum socialism to feed an expanding world population.

[37] According to Alexander Yanov (a former member of the U.S.S.R. Union of Writers), I. Shevstov's "black" novels (such as *Vo imia ottsa i sina* [Moscow: Moskovskii rabochii, 1970] got past the censor only with the support of then Politburo member D. S. Poliansky, who Yanov says wanted to become a new Stalin and came close in 1970 to supplanting Kosygin. See Alexander Yanov, *Détente after Brezhnev* (Berkeley, Calif.: Institute of International Studies, University of California, 1977), pp. 52–53, 65. Yanov cites a number of "right-wing" *samizdat* publications that link "black" with "red," propagating Russian or Soviet causes as against Zionism and détente.

Solzhenitsyn's September 5, 1973, *Letter to the Leaders of the Soviet Union.* He called on the Soviet government to "transfer the center of attention and the center of national activity (the center of settlement, the center of aspirations of youth) from distant continents, and even from Europe, nay, even from the South of our country, to its Northeast." He added that "such a relocation will sooner or later lead to our removing our control over Eastern Europe. Also, there can be no question of holding any borderland nation within the territory of our country, by force." All this would require a refocusing of energies from external to internal tasks. By removing the Marxist-Leninist ideology from the status of a state religion, the Soviet Union could also reduce the impetus for foreign expansion and one of the sources of Sino-Soviet conflict. By developing Russia's resources and returning to more rustic values, the Soviet Union could reduce her dependence on foreign technology.

Solzhenitsyn's letter provoked other Soviet dissidents to specify their positions. Sakharov, in a fourteen-page essay dated April 3, 1974, gave qualified acceptance to Solzhenitsyn's positions on Eastern Europe and the non-Russian minorities of the Soviet Union, but came down strongly against his "economic isolationism, in supplementation of military [and] political . . . isolationism." The only legitimate form of isolationism, Sakharov wrote, was to refrain from "foisting our socialist messianism on other countries, to put an end to secret or open instigation of discord on other continents, to stop exporting deadly weapons." Thus, Sakharov opposed not only autarky but what is termed in this study a forward strategy in the Third World. Indeed, Sakharov worried lest Solzhenitsyn's "call for patriotism" strengthen predispositions "in a significant part of the Russian people and a segment of the leaders of the country" toward "Great Russian nationalism linked with a fear of falling into dependence on the West and of democratic transformations." Sakharov granted that Solzhenitsyn's posture was more defensive than Stalin's but said his "mistakes" could be "dangerous." Sakharov renewed his own earlier appeals for a strategy of global interdependence, affirming that none of the basic problems of the Soviet Union or other countries could be resolved "at the national level."

The Marxist historian dissident Roy Medvedev also responded, in a nineteen-page essay in May 1974, rejecting many of Solzhenitsyn's more inward-looking recommendations, including those on Siberia and the "border nations." But even Medvedev revealed a nationalistic concern that the Russian people had not been accorded appropriate opportunities to develop their own national and cultural distinctiveness. He therefore suggested that a capital for the Russian Republic be established separate from the capital of the Soviet Union.[38]

Some autarkists have a deep confidence in the internal resources of Soviet power—the raw materials it controls and can exploit, the quality of its ideology and leadership. But others believe that these resources must be husbanded, not squandered on trade with outsiders for nonessentials.[39] And some object to the costs of stationing Soviet troops in Eastern Europe or farther afield and to the subsidies needed to keep some allies afloat.

Some recall that Soviet industrialization was accomplished in the 1930s with very little foreign trade.[40] Soviet Russia developed its economy and emerged victorious in the Great Patriotic War relying primarily upon its own resources. Stalin, when the war ended, wanted each East European country to replicate the Soviet experience, creating an industrial base and a proletarian society. Self-sufficient development rather than a division of labor in Eastern Europe was encouraged by Moscow even after 1949, when CEMA was founded, for some countries would otherwise have remained agrarian in their ideological outlook. Soviet efforts to promote a division of labor since the early 1960s, the autarkist might note, have aggravated nationalist sentiments in East Europe.

What political factors undergird autarkist attitudes? The autarkist learns from Marxist-Leninist dialectics that conflict within and among capitalist societies is inevitable. Wars of national liberation against capitalist imperialism are also probable if not inevitable. Struggle between socialism and capitalism is foreordained. All this

---

[38] For citations and further analysis of the Solzhenitsyn letter and responses generated by it, see Frederick C. Barghoorn, *Détente and the Democratic Movement in the USSR* (New York: The Free Press, 1976), pp. 55–80; also Brovkin, "The Changing Dimensions of Dissent in The USSR (1965–1975)," p. 7.

[39] Marshall Goldman cites the case of Minister for Petroleum V. D. Shashin cutting back in May–June 1974 on Soviet commitments of petroleum exports to Japan in order to preserve valuable national resources. Goldman also finds strains on the theme of "socialism in one country" manifested, for example, in Professor K. Suvorov's essay in *Pravda* (December 18, 1975) calling for a policy to "ensure Soviet economic independence from the world capitalist economy." Reviewing economic history since Peter the Great, Goldman finds many cases when Russian rulers deepened their material dependency on the West but then retreated precipitously. Goldman concurs with the assessment here, however, that such a withdrawal in present circumstances would be more painfully dislocating and politically awkward than in earlier decades or centuries. See Marshall I. Goldman, "Autarchy or Integration—the U.S.S.R. and the World Economy," in *Soviet Economy in a New Perspective*, pp. 81–96.

[40] Even under Stalin's forced industrialization program, the Soviet economy was not more autarkic than other major systems buffeted by the Great Depression. See Michael R. Dohan, "The Economic Origins of Soviet Autarky 1927/28–1934," *Slavic Review*, vol. 35, no. 4 (December 1976), pp. 603–35.

sets sharp limits on the degree to which it is desirable or feasible to rely upon nonsocialist regimes and countries as partners in trade or the maintenance of international peace. Sooner or later, the world will be transformed in ways that emulate the Soviet model. In the meantime, it is dangerous to become interdependent with that world.[41]

Many autarkists have a deep distrust of foreign governments and peoples, flowing from a reading of history and current events which stresses the unreliability of partners not subject to Moscow's control. Indeed, some autarkists doubt the solidity of the social foundations of Communist rule in the Soviet Union and Eastern Europe. Believing that even these people may waver and succumb to the blandishments of Western life styles, autarkists prefer to insulate the peoples of the "socialist commonwealth" from undue contacts with Westerners and bourgeois Third Worlders.[42]

In short, many autarkists are also autarchists, gravitating toward a Stalinist or neo-Stalinist camp. They favor a whole range of policies at home and abroad harking back to the rigid and inward-looking premises of the late 1930s and late 1940s.[43]

The most outspoken autarkists have been Great Russian nationalist dissidents whose arguments recall those of Slavophiles against Westernizers in the last century.[44] But their sentiments presented mainly in *samizdat* probably resonate not only among many common Russian citizens but also among some officials fighting a rear-guard battle against the more officially acceptable, nonautarkist positions.[45]

---

[41] Whatever one may think of the premises, this conclusion is certainly more logical than that of the centrists, who contend that capitalism is disintegrating and aggressive but that, in the meantime, détente and trade with the West should be cultivated.

[42] An otherwise liberal Muscovite told the author in 1969 that Soviet intervention in Czechoslovakia was justified because the Dubček reforms there amounted to a stab in Russia's back.

[43] Suvorov's article in *Pravda* invoked Stalin as the one who set out the idea of economic independence, but this reference was deleted in an account released by the Soviet Embassy in London on January 13, 1976. See Goldman, "Autarchy or Integration—the U.S.S.R. and the World Economy," p. 85.

[44] The editor of *Veche* denied that his journal represented "extreme chauvinist views. We in no way intend to downgrade the achievements of other nations. We want only the strengthening of Russian national culture, patriotic traditions in the spirit of the Slavophiles and Dostoevsky, the affirmation of the originality and greatness of Russia." V. N. Osipov in *Sobranie dokumentov samizdata, Arkhiv Samizdata*, vol. 8, AC no. 586 (Munich: Radio Liberty, March 1, 1971), p. 1. Though Osipov declared that his journal did not touch "political questions" and was distributed openly, he was arrested in 1974.

[45] On the varieties of nationalist, culturalist, religious, and historical concerns in the Soviet Union—officially approved, officially tolerated, or dissident—see the discussion by Jack V. Haney, Thomas E. Bird, and George L. Kline in *Slavic Review*, vol. 32, no. 1 (March 1973), pp. 1–44.

The xenophobia of many Great Russian autarkists, like the anti-cosmopolitanism of the late Stalin years, has heavy anti-Semitic overtones.[46] But attacks on Zionism seem part of a larger fear, that Mother Russia may be drowned in a sea of non-Slavic peoples threatening to make Russians a distinct minority in the U.S.S.R.[47] Still others, like the officers who noted the heavy costs of administering the borderlands of the tsarist empire, may object to the costs—political as well as economic—of managing and subsidizing the socialist commonwealth.[48] Russian autarkists also claim that the Russian Republic bore the largest share of human and economic sacrifice in the wars in which Soviet power has been extended. If the U.S.S.R. is the prison of nations, some Russians feel that they have been its prime victims.

Extreme autarkists might feel (with Solzhenitsyn) that Russia can get along without Eastern Europe or even without some republics of the U.S.S.R. For all practical purposes, however, high officials must assume the continued existence of the U.S.S.R. as a unitary state and its hegemony over Eastern Europe and Outer Mongolia. To surrender the border republics of the U.S.S.R. or the string of compliant regimes along Soviet frontiers would be almost unthinkable, even for the most resolute Russian Communist autarkist.

But these same officials may look at unrest in Western Europe, in the border republics of the U.S.S.R., and in dissident movements in Soviet Russia and conclude that the potential gains from trade or security negotiations with the West count for little as against their disruptive impact on the domestic security of the Warsaw Pact nations. The autarkist finds abundant quotations in the works of Western advocates of "bridge-building" and "controlled nuclear war" to buttress the most alarmist interpretations of Western intentions. He studies the content of Western radio broadcasts and concludes that their reduction of overt Cold War propaganda merely represents a more subtle and insidious effort to erode Communist power. He looks

[46] For an example from the official literature, see Iurii Ivanov, *Ostorozhno: Sionism!* (Moscow: Politizdat, 1969).

[47] Some specialists believe that the official census may overstate the Russian population by 5 to 10 percent to obscure the fact that Russians already make up less than half the total population. But as Robert C. Williams has pointed out to the author, present demographic trends ensure that Russians will remain the most populous nationality for decades to come. They amounted to less than half the population before World War I, but increased proportionately when many border areas fell away after the war.

[48] Stationing troops in Poland, for example, was considerably more costly per man than in regions of comparable size within Russia. See military budgets available in the Slavic Room, Library of Congress.

at the warhead gap of the 1970s and the intimations of Chinese-American entente and concludes that détente has achieved little for Soviet security. He looks at the low level of U.S.-Soviet trade and the human-rights demands which Washington asserts as the quid pro quo for more trade and concludes that the Soviet Union should better rely on its own resources, ample even without injections of outside technology.

As indicated earlier, some Soviet officials have made clear their concern to preserve the natural resources of the Soviet Union. To be sure, the gains in hard currency and the political leverage that may accrue to the sale of oil and other raw materials abroad provide a strong incentive to continue such exports. (Moscow even abrogated oil-delivery contracts to some of its allies when world prices climbed in the mid-1970s and insisted upon upward revisions in prices to be paid for deliveries despite multiyear contracts and plans already concluded.) Participation of foreign firms in Soviet extraction and production activities also complicate efforts to hold back from international trade in raw materials, machines, and services. Nonetheless, the 1970s have witnessed the rise of many voices, increasing in volume, demanding the preservation of the natural patrimony.[49]

We should be clear, however, that a strategy to preserve resources and to enhance self-sufficiency is not necessarily tantamount to isolationism. Some economic autarky could be rationalized as a condition for a more outgoing foreign policy. Moscow, no less than Washington, probably reasons that its ability to function independently in world affairs and to lead a coalition of like-minded powers depends upon a high degree of economic self-sufficiency. In Moscow, as in Washington, leaders must also ask what price they can or should pay for self-sufficiency. At what price should they trade some security for an easier road to economic growth or environmental enhancement?[50]

The Mixed or "Standard" Model

The dominant theme in Soviet policy since the death of Stalin has been the pursuit of détente and trade with the West. But the other policy orientations have also been present, becoming more salient or receding with circumstances of time and place. Thus, the

[49] See Goldman, "Soviet Raw Materials: Production and Exports."

[50] See also Mason Willrich et al., *Energy and World Politics* (New York: Free Press, 1975), pp. 91–92, 210; and Keohane and Nye, *Power and Interdependence*, p. 239.

quest for improved relations with the West has been conducted in ways designed to ensure the basic self-reliance of the Soviet camp while permitting the Kremlin to press its propaganda campaigns and physical presence in the Third World, even while paying occasional obeisance to the globalist ideals of many Westerners.

In short, elements of each approach have found their way into Soviet policies. Sometimes this has amounted to sending different messages to different audiences, for example, encouraging Arab oil producers to embargo the West while simultaneously fanning the hopes of Western businessmen for mutually advantageous trade deals with the Soviet Union. Sometimes there has been an adjustment of priorities to accommodate moments of opportunity—the subordinating of most other policy concerns to the achievement of a series of U.S.-Soviet agreements in the summer of 1971, for example. At other moments a single speech (particularly a long one, such as Brezhnev's main report to the Twenty-fifth Party Congress) may contain policy recommendations that appear to be logically inconsistent. Similarly, Brezhnev's lengthy responses to questions posed by *Le Monde* during his visit to Paris in 1977 permitted him to assert Soviet support for a variety of conflicting approaches to world affairs, from détente to forward strategy, qualifying each so as to diminish the more egregious contradictions.[51]

The mixed or logically inconsistent model probably represents the standard Soviet response to the dilemmas of interdependence and security. The four distinct schools sketched here may be seen as canonical variations of a mixed model that tries to placate contending factions within the U.S.S.R. while keeping options open to whatever contingencies emerge. This mixed approach also permits wishful thinking to persist instead of the making of painful choices that may turn out to be based on incorrect assumptions. The internal contradictions in Soviet policy, it would seem, are not more glaring than those in the Nixon-Ford policies which called simultaneously for a Project Interdependence and a Project Independence. A believer in dialectics might comment that the essence of all reality is the unity and mutual struggle of opposites.

[51] Brezhnev called for joint efforts to make détente irreversible; stressed the globalist assumption that peace is indivisible, warning that the interconnection (*vzaimosviaz'*) among different parts of the world made it easy for local conflicts to become general; affirmed Moscow's intention to support just struggles in Africa for freedom and independence and against racism and apartheid; but denied any Soviet responsibility for the economic consequences of colonialism or neocolonialism in the Third World. See *Izvestiia*, June 16, 1977.

3
Competing Trends

All of us . . . are aboard the same spaceship which, by the way, does not have any exhaust valves.

DZHERMEN M. GVISHIANI, 1973

You feed your allies; we'll feed ours.

SOVIET VISITOR TO WASHINGTON, 1976

Having identified the major tendencies in Soviet thinking about interdependence and security, can we also identify the trends in Soviet words and deeds which suggest the relative strengths of each school in recent years? This task is made difficult not only by the necessity of reading between the lines of Soviet statements, but also by the intertwining of optimism and pessimism, confidence and inferiority complex, self-righteousness and insecurity in Soviet thinking.

Taking these conundrums into account, we conclude that confidence underlies an eversion syndrome, one oriented toward opening the Soviet Union to the world; insecurity underlies an orientation toward inversion. Recognition of the complexity of contemporary problems—existential as well as technological—is also conducive to seeking cooperative solutions across frontiers, while those who insist on the feasibility of simpler solutions, who deny complexity and affirm old dogmas, tend to look inward or prefer resolute pressure against imperialism rather than accommodation. They probably fear the West as much as they trust their own resources, but they insist that the needs of the Soviet Union can best be met by reliance on the country's natural wealth, its traditions, and Communist ideology.

Confidence and admission of complexity, in short, correlate with the globalist tendencies toward détente and trade, while anxiety and dogmatism belong more to the autarkist and forward-strategy orientations.

Each of the major tendencies in Soviet perspectives today has roots in the ancient dichotomy between Westernizers and their op-

Dzhermen M. Gvishiani was deputy chairman of the U.S.S.R. State Committee for Science and Technology.

ponents. Proponents of détente and trade with the West, like Peter the Great, may be ranked among those Russian rulers who have sought a window on the West to bring modern technology and work habits to Russia without altering the country's political and economic modes of operation very much; official proponents of globalism, in contrast, probably hope not only to acquire modern technology but also to modernize and thereby salvage the Soviet system; other globalists, such as Andrei Sakharov, are humanists whose visions outstrip all parochial perspectives. A convergence of Soviet and Western energies, and a blending of the strengths of the now opposed systems, he has argued, would benefit all humanity, even as it transformed the Soviet Union. Autarkists, by comparison, resemble more the Slavophiles who urged Russia to focus on its own resources—spiritual and material—while forward strategists recall the Russian officials and propagandists who used Pan-Slavism as a justification and instrument for expansion, even beyond the realm of Slavdom.[1]

Windows to the West: Confidence plus Complexity

The centrist positions taken by Khrushchev and Brezhnev have assumed that the Soviet Union has become a superpower, accepted virtually as the equal of the United States. Within a few years of taking the helm, both men staked their careers on the proposition that it was both desirable and feasible to strike major accords with Washington and other Western governments that would advance the security, economic, and other interests of their regime and the Soviet state. Though basically confident about the capacity of the Soviet Union to hold its own in world affairs, they also admitted the utility of East-West collaboration in many realms. Such collaboration, they assumed further, could be conducted in ways that did not undermine the legitimacy of Communist rule at home or in Eastern Europe.[2]

Thus, the Twenty-fourth and Twenty-fifth Party Congresses gave special attention to the "Peace Programme" on which Brezhnev has based his career and reputation. "Visits" of comrades Brezhnev,

---

[1] As Marx put it in 1849, writing of Hungary and Pan-Slavism: "Panslav unity is either pure visionariness or—more likely—the Russian knout." See Karl Marx and Friedrich Engels, *The Russian Menace to Europe*, Paul W. Blackstock and Bert F. Hoselitz, eds. (Glencoe, Ill.: The Free Press, 1952), p. 63. The dangers posed by Pan-Slavism to non-Slavs are discussed on pp. 56–90.

[2] On the Khrushchev period, see Lincoln P. Bloomfield, Walter C. Clemens, Jr., and Franklin Griffiths, *Khrushchev and the Arms Race* (Cambridge, Mass.: M.I.T. Press, 1966); also the analysis of Khrushchev's memoirs in Clemens, "*Kto Kovo?* The Present Danger, as Seen from Moscow," pp. 4–9.

Kosygin, and Podgorny to the United States and other countries are listed as entries in the 1973 *Diplomatic Dictionary.* While President Ford jettisoned the word "détente" in the 1976 elections, Soviet authors writing in *World Economics and International Relations* that year continued to use it (*razriadka*)—always positively—as often as eight times on a single page![3]

Confidence in the growing power and authority of the Soviet Union underpins Soviet praise of Brezhnev's peace policy. SALT and other arms negotiations now proceed on the basis of "equal security." The correlation of forces turns ever more to favor the socialist camp. Instead of merely criticizing Western life styles, Soviet writers in the mid-1970s assert the virtues of the Soviet life style and the superiority of socialist over capitalist civilization.

Concurrent with Moscow's apparent optimism there are strains in the Soviet press suggesting that Kremlin officials may be whistling in the dark, seeking to keep up their own spirits or those of others in the face of mounting uncertainties. If virtually every article in a single issue of the American journal *Foreign Policy* dotes on the paradoxes and policy dilemmas of today's world,[4] so many Soviet authors recognize and affirm the growing complexity—*slozhnost'*—of contemporary international issues.[5] Such complexities are underscored in informal remarks by Soviet scholars in different fields even more forcefully than in their published works.[6] They emerge also in recent films for

---

[3] For analysis of this term and its political significance, see Walter C. Clemens, Jr., "The Impact of Détente on Chinese and Soviet Communism," *Journal of International Affairs*, vol. 28, no. 2 (1974), pp. 133–57.

[4] See Walter C. Clemens, Jr., content analysis of the fall 1972 issue of *Foreign Policy*, no. 10 (Spring 1973), pp. 182–85.

[5] French Socialist leader F. Mitterand and IMEMO director Nikolai N. Inozemtsev agreed in a 1976 colloquium on the "complex [*kompleksnom*] character of the present crisis of capitalism, on the interweaving [*perepletenii*] in it of economic, social-political, moral-political processes and events." See *MEMO*, no. 8 (August 1976), pp. 145–48 at p. 145. In the same issue, O. Bykov and V. Zagladin write about complexities and contradictions in the present state of East-West relations, but stress the ways in which détente helps both peace and social progress. Bykov praises the American people for rejecting isolationism and for wishing to play a constructive role in the world, basing his analysis on a Harris poll conducted for the Chicago Committee on Foreign Relations in 1975. See O. Bykov, "SShA i real'nosti mezhdunarodnoi razriadki," pp. 28–38 at p. 35, and V. Zagladin, "Vydaiushchiisiia vklad v delo mira i progressa," pp. 4–27.

[6] Increasing use by Soviet scholars of quantitative methods in history and the social sciences seems to contribute to this trend. The testing of alternative hypotheses is made more feasible as computers and large amounts of data become available for cross-tabulations. There is also a strong pressure for consideration of alternate hypotheses if available data do not support ideologically anticipated answers.

Soviet analysts in recent years have noted that there exist not just classes within Soviet society, but groups, strata, and other subunits with particularistic

general Soviet audiences emphasizing the complexities of the human psyche and today's world rather than etching an idealized hero in the spirit of socialist romanticism.[7]

Soviet authors writing on world affairs use with ever greater frequency the prefix *vzaimo*—"reciprocal," "mutual," or "inter," as in "reciprocal gain," "mutual advantage," "interaction," and "interdependence." Sometimes these usages are politically neutral, reflecting merely the greater *slozhnost'* of international affairs.[8] At other times these terms portray the positive interaction of the U.S.S.R. with its allies or Third World countries, or the negative interaction within Western nations or between them and the Third world. On some occasions, however, these terms are applied to Soviet-Western relations, most frequently in the sphere of trade ("mutual advantage") but sometimes in more cosmic ways ("interdependence" in solving common problems). Such usages rarely occur in the provincial party press or military publications, but they can be found in the magazine *Young Communist*, in *Izvestiia*, and—most important—in Brezhnev's major speeches.[9] The Soviet world view has come some distance since

---

interests. Agitators have therefore been urged to take a "differentiated" (*differentsirovannyi*) approach in relating to diverse groups. See George Breslauer, "The Soviet System and the Future," *Problems of Communism*, vol. 25, no. 2 (March–April 1976), pp. 66–71.

[7] *Romans o vliublënnykh*, for example, shows the problems that arise when a young marine presumed dead (lost on a Siberian ice field) returns to find his fiancée married to an old friend; it shows why he might go through periods of depression and become deranged; why he might even break socialist property and fight with good-natured comrades trying to help him. (Not until *Coming Home* [1978] did Hollywood produce an insightful study of comparable problems faced by veterans returning from Vietnam.) Another recent film, *Bag* (1971) shows how hateful were the followers of Wrangel in the Russian civil war, and (in Part Two), how pathetic when they fled to Turkey.

For examples of how the changing role of the hero and the pedagogical functions of the arts can be discussed from a liberal standpoint in the official Soviet press, see the essays by Alexander Yanov first published in *Iskusstvo kino* (1972) and *Novyi mir* (1972), translated in *International Journal of Sociology*, vol. 6, no. 2–3 (Summer-Fall 1976) pp. 75–175.

[8] Gravitating from a neutral position toward a positive use of interdependence in East-West relations, some Soviet authors speak of a dialectical interaction and interdependency between military détente (arms control) and political détente. The first is possible without the second but will lack the solid foundations which need also to be built up.

This recalls France's support of "moral disarmament" in the years between the world wars when Moscow championed "material disarmament." The Brezhnev regime has usually sought whichever it could get first on acceptable terms, trying to develop the other as well.

[9] See G. Sviatov, "Ogranichenie vooruzhenii: dostizheniia i problemy," *Molodoi Kommunist*, March 1975, pp. 101–07; V. Osipov, "The Logic of Coexistence"; *Materialy XXV s"ezda.*

the late Stalin years when "cosmopolitanism" was defined as a reactionary, rootless, antipatriotic, and hypocritical bourgeois outlook.

Vzaimo and *slozhno* both hint at the growing interdependence of things and processes in the world of today. Like multivariate analysis in science, they imply a deepening awareness of the multifaceted quality of reality and growing doubts about the validity of monocausal explanations. The world is not dichotomous but multivariate; it is not and will never be at some final state but always in flux. Even the word "contradiction" (*protivorechie*) sometimes takes on a new significance in this context, suggesting that old myths must be dropped and new realities squarely faced.

Those who admit complexity and are not afraid of East-West contact are also more likely to borrow Western terminology and methodology, even in the social sciences. Westernisms generally enter spoken Russian before finding their way into the written language. Thus, Soviet strategists adopted the acronym for "multiple independently targeted reentry vehicle" and have for years used *MIRV* and *MIRVovat'* (an infinitive) in conversation, though their published works use only the rather lengthy corresponding Russian terms. Many words long used in the written Russian seem, in the era of détente, to have achieved much greater currency, almost supplanting their Russian equivalents: *lider* and *liderstvo* ("leadership," without the Stalinist overtones of *rukovodstvo*); *biznesmen* (less pejorative than *kapitalist* or *torgovets*); and a Russified transliteration of "management," perhaps more scientific-sounding than the traditional Russian term, *upravlenie*.[10] A Soviet analysis of *transnational'nye monopolii* (in *MEMO*, no. 1 [January 1978], pp. 26–36) speaks of *kvota* and *autsaider* ("quota" and "outsider") in the oil business; *litsenziia* for arms production; *korruptsiia* and *al'lians*, a non-Russian word for an unholy alliance between government and business; and commends the socialist *al'ternativa* of a gradual coming together of national economies.

In an era of improved East-West relations, *amerikanskie finansisty* and "representatives of big business" (*predstaviteli krupnogo biznesa*) or the "business world" (*delovogo mira*) can be partners with Soviets in "diverse forms of productive cooperation" (*razlichnye formy*

---

[10] One character in a 1972 play is listed as the "commercial director of a (Soviet) firm" (*kommercheskii direktor firmy*). See Ignatii Dvoretskii, "Chelovek so storony," *Teatr* (October 1972). See also the argument by V. Moev that to comprehend labor turnover problems it is necessary to see their "complicated and multifaceted interconnections [*slozhnye i mnogoobraznye vzaimosviazi*]. . . ." (Symposium on "Working Class and Literature" in *Druzhba narodov*, no. 3 [1970], p. 265.)

proizvodstvennogo kooperirovaniia),[11] and "détente" may be rendered *detent* as well as by *razriadka*.[12] And, as dissent becomes more prominent, Soviet spokesmen speak of *disidenty* as well as *inakodumaiushchie* ("those who think differently"). Borrowing more from Europe than from the United States, Soviets also speak of *politologiia* ("political science"), but for years Moscow has had its own term (responding to Herman Kahn and others) *futurologiia*; more belatedly, the Soviet Union also had cultivated an equivalent to Kremlinology: *beldomologiia*—"White House watching."

And in a time of *detent* it is *OK* to play *dzhaz* as well as to say it. Meanwhile, *kosmonavty* and astronauts have a common language from "start" to "stop."[13] Like the Académie française, Russian traditionalists may prefer to keep the language and minds of the people free from foreign influences, but they can hardly root out the many imports already established in Soviet dictionaries.[14]

What, in this context, do we make of growing Soviet use of *vzaimozavisimost'* ("interdependence") and, more particularly, the claim that this idea was implicit in Lenin's affirmation that every people lives in a state and that all states form part of a global system?[15] If the term has been baptized, or, more properly, Leninized,

---

11 Iu. Kapelinskii, "Perspektivy Sovetsko-Amerikanskikh ekonomicheskikh otnoshenii," *MEMO*, no. 8 (August 1973), especially p. 14. For a discussion of the complex picture of American life being presented by Soviet journalists, see S. Frederick Starr, "The Soviet View of America," *The Wilson Quarterly*, vol. 1, no. 2 (Winter 1977), pp. 106–117.

12 From the verb meaning to pull apart, this noun was used first of all in a typographical sense: to create emphasis by separating letters. It seems to have first appeared in Soviet dictionaries in a political sense only in 1960. See Clemens, "Impact of Détente on Chinese and Soviet Communism," vol. 28, p. 134.

13 Three terms beginning with *start* (as an adjective) are given in a military dictionary: *Tolkovoi slovar' voennykh terminov* (Moscow: Voenizdat, 1966).

14 Many new words in Russian and Western languages are variations on common prefixes such as "auto" (*avto*), "agro," "Afro"; but others reflect technological innovations in the West: *akvalang* ("aqualung") or the computer language ALGOL (praised in the Soviet press for its universality); there are also political terms such as *lobbist*; and more general words such as *model'* and even *modern*, both entering Soviet usage in the mid-1960s. The verb "program" comes out *zaprogrammirovat'* and is illustrated by a 1967 quotation from the Soviet press saying that the *New York Times* has so "programmed" many readers that they think "news is not news, a fact is not a fact . . . unless it is published in the *New York Times*." See *Novye slova i znachenie slovar'* (*spravochnik po materialam pressy i literatury 60-kh godov*) (Moscow: Sovetskaia entsiklopediia, 1971).

In the computer field the rather awkward Russian *elektronno vychislitel'naia mashina* can be abbreviated EVM, but the more common usage is simply *kompiuter*, with its *supervaizer*, *printer*, and *terminal*. An IBM card is a *perforirovannaia kartochka*—perforated card. Another handy device is the *kal'kuletor* or, the older term, *schetnaia mashina*.

15 See Sergiyev, "Bourgeois Theories of 'Interdependence' Serve Neocolonialism," pp. 103, 109–110.

does this portend Soviet embrace of East-West or even global interdependence? This is possible, but the basic framework of Soviet use in the mid-1970s has been to "expose" the "sham" interdependence now being foisted on the Third World by the West and to propagate genuine interdependence as practiced in CEMA and offered by the socialist states to the developing countries.

Rooting Soviet discussion of interdependence in Lenin's works has so far provided more a vehicle for anti-Western propaganda than a conduit to fresh, creative approaches to North-South or East-West problems. Leninization of interdependence theory has been stunted from the outset by its claim that socialist integration in CEMA is the model for all such relations. If the socialist commonwealth offers the only pure framework for international economic relations, the nonaligned or Western nations are condemned to lag behind this ideal state. (Furthermore, as Soviet spokesmen concede, even in CEMA there remains much to achieve in the realm of "perfecting the mechanism" of integration.) Though the Soviet government believes "there must be an integral system of international economic relations," its "relations with individual units of that system" are shaped by "class" considerations.[16]

Soviet writers rule out most Western theorizing as illegitimate and self-serving, reserving to Moscow all right to pontification ex cathedra. They assert, in effect, that it is for the socialist camp to produce theories about world development and interaction, when and if it chooses to do so, rather than for outsiders led by greed or misled by ideological illusions. But since Moscow has contributed as yet virtually nothing to the resolution of global problems such as food and population, it might appear that all efforts to cope with these issues should be suspended until the Kremlin feels they have become critical.

Thus, the Leninization of interdependence *at present* fits into its forward strategy in the Third World better than the détente and trade negotiations with the West or some globalist approach. It *could* presage a more liberal turn in the future, however, just as Soviet publication of Leninist scriptures supporting arms control in 1959–1964 helped justify a more serious approach to arms negotiations in the early 1960s.[17]

Indeed, the perception gap between Westerners and Soviet thinkers with respect to interdependence might be more readily closed than Russia's lag in computer and other technologies. Communications and

---

[16] Ibid., p. 110.

[17] See Clemens, *The Superpowers and Arms Control*, pp. 85–86; and "Lenin and Disarmament," *Slavic Review*, vol. 23, no. 3 (September 1964), pp. 504–25.

dialogue helped improve the understanding of both sides on arms control in the 1950s and 1960s. Analogous achievements may still be made concerning interdependence in the 1970s.

The very act of criticizing Western studies such as those by the Club of Rome compels Soviet scholars to consider the arguments and data that they contain. The alert Soviet reader, even if he has no access to the original, may add important data from his own information base to the limited and often distorted material reported in Soviet publications.

The Soviet press has responded with basically negative criticism to most Western environmental analyses, such as those sponsored by the Club of Rome. But if more than ten major projects have already been undertaken in the West to study global problems, as noted in *Kommunist*, why is the Soviet Union without serious counterpart studies.[18] Soviet scholars are supposed to be more enlightened, since they have the Marxist ability to sniff out the trends of history. But they are forced into the position of sniping at major works in the West.

Trends, zigs, and zags in Western ecological analyses have been shaped primarily by independent thinking and criticism in the West, rather than by Kremlin cavils. But if we review Soviet writing from the late 1960s through the mid-1970s, it seems fair to conclude that Soviet analysts of ecological problems have gravitated toward Western globalism, even though they must carry the albatross of "no ideological coexistence with capitalism."

Historic Antagonism: Anxiety plus Dogmatism

Analysis of Soviet semantics in the 1970s points to an important ambiguity or, perhaps, contradiction. It uncovers trends supportive of greater accommodation with the West, but it also finds strong forces within the U.S.S.R. calling for a more militant posture, either sealing Russia off from outside contagion, urging imperial expansion, or both.

The idea of peaceful competition with the West has for decades been expressed by the term *sorevnovanie*—connoting the rivalry of athletes rather than the fundamentally hostile *konkurentsiia*, with its connotation of a fight to the finish among antagonistic firms.[19] In the

---

[18] V. Zagladin and I. Frolov, "Global'nyie problemy sovremennosti," *Kommunist*, no. 16 (November 1976), pp. 93–104. Dr. Nikolai N. Inozemtsev commented in May 1977 that the studies of such Western groups as the Hudson Institute and the Club of Rome want to change the world, whereas the IMEMO wants only to know what changes are more likely.

[19] *Slovar' russkogo iazika*, S. I. Ozhegov, ed. (Moscow, 1953), defines *sorevnovanie* as *sostiazanie* which, in turn, is defined as "sporting *sorevnovanie* for su-

mid-1970s, however, many Soviet writers posited a relationship between the Soviet and Western worlds of *protivoborstvo*—a term for "struggle" or "wrestling" that could suggest a more active competition than that officially espoused during most of the years since Stalin's death. In the same vein, some Soviet journals spoke of an *istoricheskii spor* ("historical dispute") with capitalism, a term that Russian readers would find excessive if applied, for example, to the perennial rivalry of Moscow and Leningrad.

While some Soviet uses of "contradiction" imply a more subtle approach to the complexities of modern life, the term is also employed with its most dogmatic and hostile connotations. A 1975 essay quotes both Brezhnev and the 1971 CPSU Congress to the effect that contradictions among imperialists are growing and remain an ineradicable and important regularity (*zakonomernost'*) of capitalist society. The reader may ask: Is long-term collaboration possible or desirable with a foe that is eating its own innards? He might well infer a negative reply. Granted that integrative processes are taking place among capitalist states and that international monopolies of new types reflect the "cosmopolitanism of capital," these do not mean that old, national imperialisms have died away. Quite the contrary. "The cards are spoiled." As geographical frontiers correspond ever less to the demarcation of interests of national financial capitals, contradictions multiply in the West.[20]

"Inter-imperialist antagonisms, generated by the very essence of monopoly capitalism, envelop the entire capitalist system of the international division of labor" with its dependent appendages in the Third World. The breaking up of this division of labor as a result of the socialist revolution and the national liberation movement is not yet complete, however, and capitalism strives to create new forms of international exploitation and colonialism.[21]

---

premacy." "Socialist *sorevnovanie*," the dictionary adds, "is an advanced method of labor, leading to a general improvement in the productivity of labor and the socialist economy." Some Soviet economists favoring decentralization of decision making spoke of *sotsialisticheskaia konkurentsiia* in the mid-1960s, but this term was soon dropped as inappropriate for socialist society. In remarks at the Kennan Institute on May 20, 1977, however, Nikolai N. Inozemtsev spoke of *konkurentsiia* between his own (IMEMO) and other Soviet research institutes.

[20] E. Pletnev, "Dvizhushchie sily mezhimperialisticheskikh protivorechii," *MEMO*, no. 3 (March 1975), pp. 11–19 at pp. 11–12.

[21] Ibid., p. 16. The question arises: If integration and international division of labor are good in the East, why are they bad elsewhere. The Soviet answer seems to be that in CEMA these processes are socialist, progressive, planned, and decided on democratically, and—as it happens—harmonious to Soviet objectives. In the West, they are the residue of exploitative relations—within and among nonsocialist countries—manipulated by dominant bourgeois circles.

This essay also affirms that within the United States and other capitalist countries, contradictions and the unfolding of the class struggle continue to shake the political superstructure, though a collapse of the present system is not in sight.[22] While America might recover from the economic crises of the mid-1970s, its low point lies ahead, for no magic tax wand could restore economic health. Indeed, "by reason of the depth and breadth of the mutually reinforcing crisis events, each interdependent with the other," the present difficulties of world capitalism could become the most serious of the post-1945 years.[23]

What is the Soviet reader to think about the practical and theoretical capabilities of the West to cope with the challenges of the 1970s? Why collaborate with a system hopelessly crippled by its economic and social base? Why not just stand by as the dying system collapses into the quicksand of history? If even "humanistic" and well-informed Western studies on interdependence are "utopian" because they can find no viable solution while capitalism endures, why bother to read and refute them? Here then is still another "contradiction" to puzzle Soviet citizens: Their leaders want to collaborate with adversaries who are not only antagonistic to progress but whose way of life is doomed to pass from the scene.

The contemptuous way in which Soviet authors treat Western approaches to interdependence and global problems implies almost an approach-avoidance syndrome in Moscow. Soviet offers to collaborate are couched in language so offensive that it almost ensures their rejection if Westerners took Soviet words at face value.

Some of this language should probably be treated as the Soviet equivalent of Fourth of July rhetoric in the United States. It may also be necessary for some Soviet leaders—perhaps Brezhnev himself—to reaffirm his roots in Leninist dogma to counterbalance their westward orientation. But official Soviet literature and *samizdat* writings also reveal the existence of what can only be viewed as hard-line chauvinism, opposed to Zionist and Western influences, and anxious to exterminate them within the Soviet Union. Some writers focus on defending Fortress Russia, while others urge its expansion into an expanded but hermetically sealed empire.

---

[22] See, for example, V. Zolotukhin, "Amerikanskaia dvukhpartiinaia sistema: sovremennye tendentsii," *MEMO*, no. 2 (February 1975), pp. 94–100. This particular essay contains much solid empirical material and thoughtful analysis embraced in a dogmatic framework.

[23] See the report on a discussion of the IMEMO Academic Council, "Ekonomicheskii krizis v mire kapitalizma," *MEMO*, no. 4 (April 1975), pp. 15–31 at p. 21.

Like Sergei Sharapov, a nationalistic journalist writing at the end of the last century, some contemporary Soviet writers manage to combine an imperial principle of limited expansionism with an isolationist one—sealing off the empire from outside. Sharapov's ideal empire (with its capital in Constantinople) would ensure Russia's strategic dominion over the West, guarantee noninterference from the West in the internal affairs of the empire, particularly in its methods of solving the Jewish and other national questions, and assure the economic and political self-sufficiency of the empire.[24]

Bizarre? Yes—then and now, but reality often becomes stranger than fiction. A 1975 Russian *samizdat* article denounced Zionist-leaning dissidents supported by the United States and other Zionist-dominated countries, "attempting by various means to subvert our country within, in order to pave the way to world domination for the children of Israel." Similarly, the heroine of a noval published in 1970 with high-level backing recalls that a U.S. journalist once told her: "We won't fight Russia. We'll destroy the Russian Communists and Soviets by peaceful means, using the younger generation. . . . We'll bring them up to think as we do." Again, a public lecture by Soviet ideological official V. Yemel'yanov in Moscow on February 7, 1973 (about the same time that *Izvestiia* published the globalist article cited above), asserted that the Jews plan "to march to world domination by stepping on the heads of other peoples. . . . World Zionism now controls 80 percent of the world economy." If the struggle against Hitler cost 20 million Soviet lives, Yemel'yanov suggested, the battle against Zionism could cost 80 million![25]

Sakharov, as noted before, has worried about the predisposition "in a significant part of the Russian people and a segment of the leaders" of the Soviet Union toward "Great Russian nationalism linked with fear of falling into dependence on the West and of democratic transformations." Looking at the same problem, Alexander Yanov suggests that speeches such as Yemel'yanov's generate an "electricity that runs from the lecturer to the audience and back again. Until then they have felt that they were at opposite poles of the system, cold and estranged, but suddenly they sense their profound inner kinship. . . . Once again they have one common enemy, one common Devil—they are united again." To understand how powerful such propaganda is in Russia "one has to know a Russian's passionate

[24] S. F. Sharapov, *Cherez polveka* (Moscow, 1901), analyzed by Alexander Yanov in *Détente after Brezhnev* (Berkeley, Calif.: Institute of International Studies, University of California, 1977), pp. 45–50.

[25] Cited ibid., pp. 49, 53.

desire to be reconciled with authority, his desire to feel and think in the same way authority feels and thinks, to love and hate the same things."[26]

In short, historic tendencies associated with Slavophilic introversion and pan-Slavic expansion live on, adumbrated in the official and unofficial press and rooted in what appear to be vested interests and popular dispositions. Translated into the language of the present analysis, this means important support both for the autarkist and forward-strategy schools, perhaps in combination.

Still, "authoritarian personalities" and anti-Semitism exist in many countries. Perhaps statements such as those which Yanov cites are merely emotional discharges from fringe elements in Soviet society? And has not one of their sponsors, Poliansky, already been defeated in his attempt to seize power and perhaps re-Stalinize the country?

All this is true, but the last battle has not yet been fought, and Soviet rulers have often incorporated the programmatic recommendations of their foes, once defeated. Moreover, the power structure as well as the latent sentiments of Soviet society may still favor a right-wing alternative.

Self-Interest: Central Committee Majority versus a New "New Class"?

Beyond semantics and sentiments, who stands to gain if one or the other tendency comes to predominate? Soviet politics under Brezhnev has become the whipping boy of *two* Central Committees, according to Alexander Yanov. One is the CPSU Central Committee plenum—the true parliament of the Soviet Union; the second is the Central Committee apparatus, 6,000 clerks on Staraia Square in Moscow headed by fifteen oligarchs—the Soviet equivalent of the U.S. executive branch.[27] The first body is dominated by local party secretaries; though selected by Brezhnev (or his staff), they defend their local and personal interests however and whenever possible. The second body is much more responsive to the will of the Politburo (whose members are nominated and elected by the Central Committee plenum).

The party prefects can have an absolute majority in the Central Committee plenum if they act in concert with two other groups: first,

---

[26] Ibid., p. 49.

[27] Ibid., p. 41.

representatives of the central economic apparatus and ministries and, second, the military-industrial complex. All three factions stand to lose if liberalization and/or détente go too far. The organizational function of the prefects could be rendered superfluous if managers acted on their own without needing to beg local CPSU secretaries to intervene in their behalf, lowering quotas, pillaging resources from other firms, establishing priorities, and so forth. Decentralization of the economy would also undercut the role of the centralized Moscow ministries. Similarly, the military-industrial complex also has cause to fear any trends that could diminish its claim to resources. Its position becomes ambiguous in a world of détente and arms control.[28] An atmosphere of confrontation does more for its resource base and prestige. These three factions might also gain support from the KGB—at least its domestic services—and ideological workers in the party, both of whom must contend with the unsettling consequences of liberalization and détente on Soviet domestic security and ideological zeal.

But other evidence (including much material provided by Yanov) suggests that the potential for conflict between these groups and the Politburo with its 6,000 clerks and other modernizing factions is more limited than he indicates. In the first place, the dividing lines are not so clearly marked, and the factions are probably much more variegated.[29] Thus, some military men probably welcome détente because it reduces the chances of a two-front war and facilitates their acccess to advanced computers, while the PRO (antirocket defense) force laments the ABM treaty. (So far, this is the only branch to have suffered visible damage from arms limitations.[30]) Second, the Central Committee plenum has never overthrown a top CPSU leader; instead, it has *approved* changes initiated from within the Politburo; its greatest initiative in this respect was to reaffirm Khruschev's tenure in 1957 against what came to be known as the antiparty group. Third, the most extreme designs of the modernizing détente-oriented Soviet leaders may well be compatible with the sectarian interests of the three groups Yanov describes. The centrist leaders probably do not contemplate such change as would displace the local prefects, nor so much decentralization that the central ministerial apparatus would

---

[28] Ibid., pp. 41, 66–67.

[29] A much more complex portrait emerges from the detailed studies edited by Thomas and Kruse-Vaucienne, *Soviet Science and Technology.*

[30] Clemens, "The Soviet Military and SALT." *Protivoraketnaia oborona* (*PRO*) is a part of *Protivovozdushnaia oborona (PVO)*, Anti-air Defense, which has apparently prospered in recent years.

become redundant, nor so much arms control that the military-industrial complex would wither on the vine. To the extent that the Politburo goes too far, it can be checked, its plans stymied and subjected to revision, but hardly compelled to alter directions by the plenum. As for the armed forces and the KGB, their top leaders at present are civilians with long-term personal connections with Brezhnev and full members of the Politburo; these are men whose attitudes make them more likely to swing their institutions to do Brezhnev's will than vice versa.

All these persons are "hooked" on Western living standards. In Yanov's words, the Western-oriented centrists running the Politburo now represent the "entire social hierarchy of Soviet society—from the middle-ranking conformist scholar who for the first time has gained the opportunity . . . openly [to acquire] original works by the French Impressionists to the hairdresser who wins prizes at a competition in Brussels."[31] Those at the top want to vitalize the Soviet economy through imports and stimuli from the West; lower ranks want to hang on to the privileged life style to which they are becoming accustomed; others, further down, may resent the new "new class" but hope to join it. According to one former insider, intangibles as well as tangibles are at issue. Secret Soviet sociological studies show that 40 to 50 percent of the educated population regularly listened to Western radio broadcasts in 1976 (compared with about 3 percent ten years before) and that nine out of ten Soviet consumers prefer imported products.[32]

Surely the perquisites of the military-industrial complex and the central ministries can also be kept aloft by directing some of the Western products now available into the special commissaries available for the Soviet elite. And if there is any trickle-down effect, surely the local prefects can also gain, albeit indirectly, from Westernization. Indeed, the hope is that, with time, ever widening circles of Soviet society will so benefit. As the Moscow Metro once symbolized a better life for the *masses*, so today the Togliatti works (where Soviet Fiats are made) suggests the promise of a better life for the *individual.* Without *both* détente and trade, how will this be possible? What sectarian, ideological concern would justify scuttling this orientation?

Moreover, the number of persons whose material interests (*zainteresovanost'*) gain from East-West ties has constantly widened

[31] Yanov, *Détente after Brezhnev*, pp. 4–5.

[32] Boris Rabbot (formerly an aide to erstwhile Central Committee member A. M. Rumiantsev), "Détente: The Struggle within the Kremlin," *Washington Post*, July 10, 1977.

in recent years. If Stalin managed to make a "big deal" with thousands of local party leaders, industrial managers, and *stakhanovites*, purchasing their support by creating a stake for them in his policies,[33] the circles of those who profit materially from the system have been steadily expanded since the mid-1950s. If a "new class" existed under Stalin and Khrushchev, a new "new class" has been generated under Brezhnev, many of whom derive their special status from the widened windows to the West. Beneath the thousand or so privileged persons at the top of the Soviet power structure, there are now tens of thousands of Soviet citizens who acquire special benefits from increased contacts with the outside world.[34]

These benefits vary with rank and opportunity, but they are esteemed at all levels. For Brezhnev it may be the privilege of receiving one or two racing cars with each visit to Paris (please, not two of the same color); for the son of Politburo member Kirill Mazurov it is the privilege of hunting elephants in Africa; for one diplomat who visited the author's home it is having the same kitchen linoleum in Moscow that one finds in Lexington, Massachusetts; for a trade union clerk or KGB operative who accompanies tourist groups abroad it is the privilege of obtaining Chanel No. 5; for a party hack described by Vladimir Voinovich it is the dream of having a "stereophonic toilet"; for almost every delegate to the West it is economizing on food to buy goods with limited hard currency and packing them so as to evade customs inspectors in Moscow; for the children of the elite it is entering the diplomatic or journalistic training institutes that help ensure a foot in foreign doors for the rest of their lives.

Common Pillars

All major tendencies within the Soviet establishment share certain common assumptions, probably including the hierarchy of foreign policy goals outlined above. The most dedicated Kremlin proponents of détente or globalism will forsake these approaches if they appear to undermine CPSU rule in the Soviet Union or Soviet controls in Eastern Europe. No Kremlin leaders welcome any course smacking of "convergence"—a blending (as Sakharov has advocated) of socialist welfare and Western democracy. "Separate roads to communism" or autonomous "Eurocommunism" they swallow only with great difficulty. At the other end of the policy spectrum, no responsible forward

[33] Vera S. Dunham, *In Stalin's Time* (Cambridge: Cambridge University Press, 1976).

[34] Yanov, *Détente after Brezhnev*, p. 3.

strategist wants a war with the United States, and no isolationist wants to seal off Russia absolutely from global movements in technology and trade.

Thus, Brezhnev's pursuit of détente and trade has been premised on the feasibility of limiting the potentially contaminating effects of increased contact with the West within the Soviet Union and Eastern Europe. His regime has also welcomed arms accords for their political and strategic value, but has generally insisted that they be verified by national—that is, nonintrusive—means. The Kremlin has sought to minimize also the intrusive impact of heightened trade and technological transfers with the West, welcoming credits and turnkey factories but cool to joint ventures that would require lasting intimate collaboration between Soviet and Western citizens.[35]

The Brezhnev regime has not endorsed autarky as desirable or feasible, but it has sought to conduct its peace policies in ways that would strengthen its hold on Eastern Europe and contain any vulnerabilities in the region to Western influences. Soviet writers assert that the West has wanted to use détente as a battering ram to knock down the walls of the socialist camp. They contend that the manifest failure of this policy is what helped occasion disenchantment with détente in Washington in 1976. The Kremlin, for its part, has made clear that if the stability of Soviet controls in Eastern Europe appears threatened, as it was in 1968, it will intervene regardless of the consequences for East-West relations. President Carter's support of the cause of human rights within the Soviet Union has also met with repeated rebuffs; the KGB arrested one activist in 1977, for example, immediately after he had asserted that Carter's stance generated a shield for Soviet dissenters.

Negotiations with the West over European arms control and East-West trade have been accompanied with continuing Soviet efforts to "perfect" the mechanisms of the Warsaw Pact and CEMA. Moscow has sought a position of strength from which to conduct such negotiations. But the Kremlin has also wavered, sometimes jettisoning the collective interests of the CEMA nations for the sake of a purchase or sale that would be of benefit primarily to the Soviet Union. Indeed, each of the members of CEMA has sometimes performed like the hunter in Rousseau's story of the stag and the hare, defecting from the grand cause to pursue a rabbit near to hand.[36]

---

[35] Even here, however, Soviet resistance seemed to slacken in the mid-1970s, perhaps because of the success of certain East European joint ventures with Western firms.

[36] Research by Sarah M. Terry indicates that Poland and other members of CEMA sometimes sell their products (for example, meat and coal) to hard-

On balance, however, the Kremlin has exuded confidence about the trends in Eastern Europe, regardless of nationalist tendencies on the part of the various governments and dissent movements in many countries. It portrays the economic relationships with CEMA as a model of interdependence based on a rational and just division of labor, a model that should inspire other nations to associate with CEMA or follow its worthy example. The Kremlin has subsidized Poland and Czechoslovakia in recent years to help them contain popular dissent. Though Soviet outlays have been substantial, Moscow has apparently reasoned that this is a small price to pay from the enormous Soviet economy for the sake of keeping quiet on its Western front.

The 1975 Helsinki Final Act has cut both ways with respect to Soviet interests in Eastern Europe. Western affirmation of the inviolability of East European frontiers may have bolstered the image of Communist regimes from Berlin to Sofia, but it may also have reduced their dependency upon Soviet armed might as the guarantee of last resort. More troublesome, the Helsinki pledge to enhance human rights and facilitate East-West exchange has stimulated dissenting demands for a relaxation of travel restrictions and for internal reform, while providing a legal foundation on which to base criticism of East European and Soviet repression of such challenges.

Having labored for more than ten years to deliver a new carrier of proletarian internationalism in the Soviet image, the Brezhnev regime finally served as midwife in 1976 to what it could only see as the illegitimate offspring of a Tito-Ceauşescu union with Italian and French Communist godparents. This new entity bearing the name "separate roads to socialism" was embraced by Soviet representatives in Berlin, despite the obvious lack of any Soviet birthmarks, only to become an orphan in press coverage within the Soviet Union and in most Soviet statements to foreign audiences. After some months in which Moscow showed increased annoyance with the independent ways of Eurocommunists, the CPSU Central Committee came out again strongly in January 1977 for proletarian internationalism and dictatorships of the proletariat, thereby rejecting the bastard child of the Berlin Conference the previous summer. Major statements by

---

currency markets even when there are shortages within the East European community and sometimes in violation of existing CEMA agreements. On the other hand, imports of modern machinery from the West have strengthened the capacity of Poland within CEMA to produce industrial goods of better quality. Since the Soviet Union has sometimes rejected East European products because their quality was inferior to that of Western products, this has added to the incentives of Warsaw, Prague, and other CEMA capitals to acquire the most modern machinery available.

Mikhail Suslov and Brezhnev on the eve of the November 1977 anniversary of the Bolshevik Revolution granted the need for some tactical flexibility by European Communists, but reaffirmed the enduring importance of the Russian revolutionary model and principled internationalism. As Brezhnev put it on November 2: "Under no circumstances may principles be sacrificed for the sake of a tactical advantage. Otherwise, as they say, you'll keep your hair but lose your head."

The Kremlin appears, at least until 1977, to have been reasonably confident of its ability to contain internal dissent. Even if the size and quality of the dissent movement have doubled or tripled in the last decade, the Politburo could reason, this presents no deep or broad-based challenge to the authority or policies of the CPSU. Though the goal of sustaining East-West détente inhibits the taking of more decisive measures against dissenters, this constraint has not yet proved onerous. A mixture of intimidation, relaxation, incarceration, and expulsion can be used to keep dissenters and oppositionists in disarray, without the use of Stalinist methods. Indeed, the Kremlin was ready in 1973 to make some concessions on Jewish emigration for the sake of improved trade between the United States and the Soviet Union but pulled back when Washington pushed too hard without offering any substantial inducement in credits or tariffs. A domestic issue in Moscow that may be sharper than any of these is consumer dissatisfaction, a problem that could be alleviated if trade relations were improved.

The Kremlin may consider that its ultimate problem is legitimacy. How far can it go in cooperation with the West without depriving the Communist movement of its raison d'être and its élan? From the mid-1950s until the mid-1970s Soviet spokesmen—including champions of détente—have reiterated the view that peaceful coexistence is another mode of waging the class struggle, that it does not imply any freezing of the world's economic-social status quo, and that it helps rather than hinders the national liberation movement and the forces of socialism and peace in the capitalist world. Coexistence in the realm of ideology is ruled out and Moscow denies that convergence of the Soviet and Western systems is even conceivable so long as both operate from contradictory property relationships. Thus, while science or even management practices in the West and the Soviet Union might bear certain resemblances, they are fundamentally different, for one serves the exploiting class and the other the common good. "Social partnerships" in which German or British workers share in the decision making and profits of private firms are just one more ploy to delay the inevitable socialist transformation of capitalist societies.[37]

At bottom, both proponents of détente and forward strategists in Moscow continue to share a world view rooted in Lenin's question: *kto kovo*—"Who will do in whom?" This zero-sum approach to policy guides them in dealing with one another, with the Soviet population generally, and with other governments. They tend to approach the dilemmas of security and interdependence intent upon exploiting the contradictions and vulnerabilities of Eastern Europe, the Third World, and the West in ways which they hope will further shift the correlation of forces to favor the Soviet-led camp of socialism. It is an approach from which Soviet power has derived important benefits but which has also engendered distrust—both at home and abroad—producing many long-term costs for the Soviet regime and preventing it from optimizing certain goals through cooperative strategies.[38]

---

[37] See V. N. Skvortsov, *Doktrina konvergentsiia i ee propaganda* (Moscow: Politizdat, 1974), pp. 33, 47.

[38] These conclusions are spelled out in Walter C. Clemens, Jr., "A Balance Sheet on Sixty Years of Soviet Foreign Policy," *Worldview*, vol. 20, no. 12 (December 1977), pp. 15–19, and vol. 21, no. 1 (January 1978), pp. 44–51.

4

Future Contingencies

Whole new ways of life—the practice of agriculture, industrialization, the storage of vast amounts of information, travel over fantastic distances, and more—await the society that can correctly engineer the division of labor of its members.

EDWARD O. WILSON, 1975

No man is an island.

JOHN DONNE, 1623.

From each according to his abilities; to each according to his needs.

KARL MARX, 1848

Interdependence is a thought and a theme that runs counter to many of our shibboleths of the past: nationalism, ethnocentrism, rugged individualism, empire, cold war, East and West with never the twain meeting, declarations of independence.

THEODORE M. HESBURGH, 1974

Which tendency, if any, will prevail in Soviet policy in the late 1970s and 1980s? Much will depend on the nature of the regime that replaces the septuagenarians now in power. Will their successors be more "Red" or "expert"—politically or technocratically oriented? Inward- or outward-looking? Liberal or Stalinist? Optimistic or fearful about the prospects of Soviet Communism in a world characterized by mounting complexity and mutual vulnerability? Depending on this assessment, they may seek to wall off the Soviet Union or plunge it deeper into bilateral, regional, or globalist cooperation.

Despite the Soviet Union's vast resources, it is likely to be influenced by the economic and environmental problems of the world more than it is able to shape them. What will be the structure of rewards and penalties (as perceived by the Soviet leaders) for with-

---

Edward O. Wilson, *Sociobiology* (Cambridge, Mass.: Harvard University Press, The Belknap Press, 1975), p. 298; John Donne, *Devotions* (1623), XVII; Karl Marx, *Communist Manifesto* (1848); Theodore M. Hesburgh, "The Problems and Opportunities on a Very Interdependent Planet," Ditchley Foundation Lecture, September 20, 1974.

drawing from on contributing to international approaches to these issues?

I will attempt to list the tendencies likely to prevail in ascending order, from the least to the most probable. This assessment, of course, is not a deterministic but a contingent forecast, considering the probable contours of the basic conditions shaping Soviet policies at home and abroad. These contours, though they will reflect long-term trends in the environment of world affairs, will be shaped also by decisions taken by individual actors all over the globe, but particularly in Washington and Moscow.

Several major caveats should be entered about such forecasts. First, they tend to be based on extrapolations from recent trends. But, in the long haul, "more of the same" may be the least likely orientation. It is almost impossible to take account of the permutations of present trends (known and unknown) resulting from the interaction of synergistic development and serendipity. The result for many societies has been "creeping catastrophies" which they did not perceive until it was too late.

Nor can we predict how individual leaders will respond to the problems and opportunities of their policy-making environment, even though they share many values of their predecessors. Differences in style are often important. Brezhnev's style, for example, has been more conducive to improved East-West relations than Khrushchev's, even though both men had similar goals and faced analogous problems.

Much depends on whether Soviet—and Western—leaders perceive the full extent of their mutual sensitivities and vulnerabilities. Thus, the U.S.S.R. may be objectively vulnerable to terrorist actions emanating from the Third World but may not perceive a need to join forces with others to contain terrorism until Soviet interests have actually been injured. To take another case, the size of the Soviet grain crop is an objective factor (though one that fluctuates yearly), while the commitment of the Politburo to providing greater supplies of meat to the Soviet consumer is a subjective one shaping the decision how much feed grain to purchase abroad.

The same data may suggest quite different implications to analysts and policy makers in Moscow and the West, depending upon whether they are given to bullish or bearish outlooks. Present difficulties—what one observer has called the mid-1977 blahs—can easily induce pessimism about the prospects for East-West cooperation. An optimist tends to give more weight to favorable possibilities over the long term, while pessimists emphasize present obstacles. Optimists think about the step-by-step process by which human interaction evolves and may express wonder at "progress" already achieved in East-West relations; "the pessimist wants the world tuned to his view instantaneously or gives up prematurely."[1] He may be incensed when U.S. industries or Soviet institutes do not bare all their work on the first meeting. Similarly, pessimistic strategists on each side tend to exaggerate the military advantages of the other side while downplaying their own, and economic forecasters will predict strong growth (for their side or the other)—with or without cooperation—depending in part on their proclivities toward optimism or pessimism.

Aware of these pitfalls, I reckon that Soviet policy makers are most likely to gravitate toward the familiar mixed model with a heavy emphasis on détente and trade with the West; least likely are the extremes of globalism and autarky. A forward strategy, I conclude, is more likely than autarky but less probable than an orientation toward détente and trade.

Globalism?

If no nation is an island unto itself, and if there are problems—military, economic, environmental, scientific—which no single country can solve alone, no matter how powerful, globalism is the tack which the world needs above all others. But it is probably the tendency least likely to dominate Soviet policy in the 1980s. Moscow could expand its horizons to endorse and act upon assumptions of global interdependence if such an orientation did not hurt or even enhanced Soviet power interests and prestige. Perhaps it could be conducted on a low-cost basis. Perhaps it would be expedient in order to maintain the Soviet image in the face of Western or Chinese advances. Perhaps it could rekindle idealism and optimism among the peoples of the Soviet Union and other socialist countries.

But this prospect is unlikely in the next decade or two for many reasons. First, there is little domestic support—elite or mass—for globalist policies implying further economic sacrifice for the long-suffering Soviet consumer. While parts of the military-industrial complex may benefit from a forward strategy in the Third World, very few bureaucratic or economic interests stand to gain from programs premised on global interdependence. Indeed, powerful forces within Soviet society probably oppose globalist cooperation: Ideologues will worry lest such programs be interpreted as forswearing

[1] See Thomas and Kruse-Vaucienne, *Soviet Science and Technology*, p. xi.

revolutionary dynamism to collaborate with the class enemy or as acceptance of Sakharov's call for convergence and parallel U.S.-Soviet action to save humanity;[2] KGB officials will warn about erosion of Communist vigilance and loyalty; some economic interests will complain about diversion of valuable resources; and military-industrial interests will object to any diminution in defense allocations.

As suggested earlier, the Kremlin and Soviet society as a whole are less empathetic to global needs than are Western governments and peoples. Thus, in emphasizing the limitations of the Soviet economy for coping with the problems of the Third World, Moscow officials imply that aid to developing countries represents a zero-sum equation in which the Soviet citizenry is often the loser.[3] The Politburo may also fear that it could not hold its own in cooperative programs with the West, because of technological backwardness, less experience, and a clumsier human touch in dealing with peoples of the Third World. Such considerations will not necessarily lead Moscow to attempt sabotage of global cooperation, but they set stiff barriers to Soviet leadership and participation in such efforts.

Other limits derive from the preference of most Third World governments for Western approaches to technology and agricultural development rather than Soviet or East European.[4] Collectivized agriculture, for example, has yielded poor results within the Soviet Union, compares unfavorably with West European and U.S. agriculture, and has produced disastrous results when tried in Mali, Tunisia, and other African countries.[5] The side effects of huge water projects built in the Soviet Union and, with Soviet aid, in Egypt also generate doubts about Soviet attempts to remold nature. Even if gigantomania achieved optimal results in the Soviet Union, it is hardly geared to the much smaller scale of the economies of most Third World countries. So long as Soviet planners are dogmatically tied to approaches that have not worked well even in the Soviet Union, why solicit their assistance if Western advice and aid are available?

And why send students to Moscow to attend Lumumba University if its degrees are testimony more to Soviet political ambitions

---

[2] The notions of convergence and superpower condominium in the Third World are denounced by L. Tolkunov, "U perednego kraia ideologicheskoi bor"by," p. 124.

[3] See *Pravda*, October 5, 1976, p. 4; also A. A. Gromyko, "The Leninist Strategy of Peace: Unity of Theory and Practice," *Kommunist*, no. 14 (September 1976), pp. 11–31.

[4] The unique approaches of Taiwan and China to agricultural and other development projects may well be more relevant to the experience of many countries of the Third World than to Western or CEMA experiences.

[5] Carl Eicher, oral communication, March 17, 1977.

than to the academic and professional achievements of the students? Having achieved power, few governments want their students to be brainwashed elsewhere or to come home with special skills in terrorism or subversion. And, having thrown off the domination of Western whites, why expose one's people to the less restrained currents of Soviet racism?

The year 1976 saw many Third World countries criticize Soviet practices in aid and trade at the United Nations Conference on Trade and Development (Nairobi, May) and the Fifth Summit Conference of Nonaligned Countries (Columbo, August). Criticism was centered on Soviet trade practices restricting less developed countries to a barter system. Such arrangements mean that revenues made by sales to the Soviet Union must be spent on Soviet goods. Many delegates to the conference in Nairobi wanted this changed and sought payments in convertible currency. Others complained that prices for industrial goods are often higher in Communist countries than in the West and that the countries of CEMA offered almost no trade preferences. One observer noted that the socialist countries absorb only 5 percent of the foreign trade of the Third World.[6]

Others have observed that, while the level of Soviet aid has increased from year to year, it is quite low in comparison with Western assistance programs, that its emphasis on showy projects does little for the man in the street (or the village path), and that long-term recipients of Soviet aid are beginning to feel the strain of repayment as their debt-servicing problems become more critical. India and Egypt may have paid more for servicing their debts in 1975 than they received in aid; Iran and Iraq have also approached zero aid. The problems in accepting Soviet aid are suggested by the steady tendency of Third World countries since 1954 to draw less than half the aid offered. The stiff terms on Soviet developmental loans and near commercial rates imposed by other CEMA countries have gone a long way toward paying for East European and Soviet imports from the developing world.[7] The value of Soviet military deliveries to Africa, meanwhile, has skyrocketed, in 1975 amounting to more than three times that of all Western states combined![8]

Soviet spokesmen had trouble coping with criticism from the

---

[6] See *The Soviet Union and the Third World: A Watershed in Great Power Policy?* U.S. House of Representatives, Report to the Committee on International Relations by the Senior Specialists Division, Congressional Reference Service, Library of Congress (Washington, D.C., May 8, 1977), pp. 114–15.

[7] Ibid., pp. 126, 152; also *Development Co-operation: 1976 Review* (Paris: OECD, November 1976), p. 64.

[8] Kenneth L. Adelman, "The Black Man's Burden," *Foreign Policy*, no. 28 (Fall 1977), pp. 86–109 at p. 93.

Third World at Nairobi, but they responded with even greater sensitivity to what Moscow called the notorious thesis of the Columbo conference that the Soviet Union should share equal responsibility with other industrialized states for coping with the economic problems of the Third World. "Are we our brothers' keepers?" Moscow's answer has been a startlingly frank *nyet*. Since the Soviet Union has not caused the damage allegedly done to the Third World by Western imperialism and neocolonialism, the Kremlin rejects any obligation to compensate for harm done in the past. As Soviet spokesmen have made clear, moreover, the Soviet Union has its own economic problems.[9] Indeed, the Soviets have indicated to their East European allies that they too must increasingly manage to swim on their own. Countries more distant ideologically must presumably depend even less on Soviet maganimity.

Another general obstacle to Soviet participation in global strategies is Moscow's penchant for bilateral actions as opposed to multilateral (outside CEMA, which it easily dominates).[10] Thus, virtually all Soviet aid programs have been conducted on a bilateral basis, though Moscow appears recently to have agreed to extend aid to Mexico, to Iraq, and possibly to Angola through CEMA channels.[11]

---

[9] The socialist countries "do not bear the responsibility for the economic backwardness which the developing countries inherited from the colonial past" and are in no way involved in the grave consequences for the less developed countries resulting from economic crises, currency collapse, and "other manifestations of production anarchy in the capitalist system." "In the Interests of Cooperation," *Pravda*, October 5, 1976, p. 4. This approach was reiterated in 1977, for example, in Brezhnev's *Le Monde* interview cited above.

[10] Moscow's preference for bilateral relations reflects among other things, its problems in competing in multilateral arenas already dominated by a number of Western (and Westernized) countries accustomed to dealing with one another. Transnational activities—multinational business enterprises, foundations, organizations of scientists, international trade union secretaries—all have their origins and locus in advanced Western countries. The increased economic specialization of advanced countries leads them to become and remain each other's best trading partners. Trade among developed market economies accounts for approximately half of the world trade, while the share of less developed countries (and of raw materials) has been declining. See Joseph S. Nye, Jr., and Robert O. Keohane, eds., *Transnational Relations and World Politics* (Cambridge, Mass.: Harvard University Press, 1972), pp. 387–388.

Among the factors accounting for these trends are modernization, decreased transportation and communication costs, pluralistic ideology, and mixed economies. The last two factors have facilitated the growth of transgovernmental and transnational activities in the West, leapfrogging the impediments which excessive centralization places in the way to any action. The Soviet Union and most of its partners in CEMA suffer precisely from their need to clear all decisions at the top.

[11] *The Soviet Union and the Third World*, p. 131. CEMA cooperative programs with Vietnam, Laos, and Finland are also reported in *New Times*, no. 27 (1977), p. 7.

The Kremlin appears to fear that it will operate at a disadvantage in multilateral arenas—it may be outvoted by hostile adversaries, and its great power will be less overwhelming than in a one-to-one confrontation. "But" as the *New York Times* has editorialized,

> energy, resources, poverty, and the search for peace and justice in the Middle East and southern Africa are issues that do not fit the bilateral mold. . . . In multilateral relations, the Soviet Union is often irrelevant, not a target of disrespect but a victim of diplomatic benign neglect.
>
> That is especially the case in economic matters. Moscow is not present at the current round of global trade negotiations. It takes no part in the reform of the international monetary system. It is mute in the "North-South dialogue." The Soviet bureaucracy is simply not prepared to risk loosening its total control over Soviet economic life and to accept the uncertainties of full participation in the multilateral world economy.

If Brezhnev's successors persist on these present paths, "they will be odd men out in an international system that may offer large benefits to those ready to risk interdependence and greater openness."[12]

Another inhibiting factor has been the lack of positive invitations to Moscow from the West to join in specific North-South cooperative endeavors. The Sahel development project, for example, sponsored by France, the United States, and six African states, emanates from the OECD, to which the Soviet Union does not belong. Why risk Soviet disruption? Why give the Kremlin an inroad on a good thing just for the sake of global cooperation? Since both sides continue to see the Third World and its resources as an arena of competition, why not keep the Sahel—or Sudan or whatever area comes under Western influence—sealed off from Soviet influences if this can be done without great difficulty? While the Sudan could become a breadbasket for much of Africa, there may be oil and other resources in the Sahel which the West could help develop—not only for the local governments, but for Western use as well.

The dark picture painted here could change drastically, however, where Moscow sees no direct challenge to its own interest from East-West collaboration in the Third World and good potential for economic or other profit. The key to such ventures lies in identifying a complementarity of interests not threatening to any of the parties.

One successful case of mutual complementarity has been the Soviet experience in helping to produce and bring natural gas from

---

[12] *New York Times*, July 10, 1977.

Iran and Afghanistan to the Soviet Union while shipping Soviet natural gas to Eastern and Western Europe. The Soviet Union has agreed to supply natural gas to a number of West European states in exchange for hard currency, steel pipe, or technology. Since 1967 Moscow has imported natural gas from Afghanistan for gas-deficit areas of the Russian Republic. But its most important foreign supplier is Iran. By a 1966 accord, Moscow has built the northern half of a pipeline from near Ahwaz, Iran, to the Soviet border at Astara and a connecting spur to Teheran; U.K. and U.S. firms built the southern half. First deliveries through this system began in 1970. Moscow has shipped Soviet natural gas to Austria (since 1968), West Germany (1973), Finland (1974), and France (1976). According to an agreement made in November 1975, substantial Iranian gas will flow to the Soviet Union through a pipeline to be built by 1981 with Western firms joining in the investment, an identical amount of Soviet gas then flowing to West Germany, France, and Austria.[13] By 1985 Western Europe may be importing a third of its natural-gas requirements from the Soviet Union. The value of Soviet natural gas exports to Europe, according to the CIA, is to rise from $200 million a year in 1975 to $2 billion by 1985.[14]

Are such arrangements mutually beneficial for the parties concerned? There are many ambiguities and paradoxes:

- Soviet sales of natural gas to Western Europe undercut the market for Algeria, a country otherwise courted by Moscow.
- Moscow pays Afghanistan much less than it does Iran for natural gas, and charges much higher prices to Western Europe and still more to its CEMA partners.[15]
- Despite some multilateral cooperation, Moscow has tried to keep Western oil and gas prospectors out of northern Iran and Afghanistan.
- Though West Europeans want natural gas from the Soviet Union, they do not want too much, and they have tried to establish maximum levels so that they do not become excessively dependent upon Soviet supplies.

---

[13] West Germany will get by far the largest share. See Arthur Jay Klinghoffer, *The Soviet Union and International Oil Politics*, pp. 129–34.

[14] U.S. Congress, Subcommittee on Priorities and Economy in Government of the Joint Economic Committee, *Soviet Economic Problems and Prospects*, p. 23.

[15] In 1973 Moscow paid Iran 29 cents a thousand cubic feet but received 39 cents from Austria, 52 cents from Poland, and 55 cents from Czechoslovakia! Ibid., p. 130.

- Since the price of Iranian gas to the Soviet Union is tied to the price of oil, increases in OPEC prices (supported by the Kremlin) add to what Moscow must pay to Iran; these charges, however, can be matched by changes in the way in which Moscow values the goods it barters to Teheran.

Throughout the Third World, the U.S.S.R. has become an important supplier of low-interest credits to assist in construction of refineries, to aid prospecting for oil, and to provide oil-field equipment. Unlike Western governments, the Kremlin has not wanted to share in ownership of facilities or in profits. Instead, repayment of loans can be made from profits generated once the facility begins operations. Moscow has often accepted local currencies or goods for repayment. The U.S.S.R. also has trained local personnel. In all these ways Moscow has provided the Soviet Union with an alternative to dependence upon Western companies and governments.[16]

Paradoxically, the sharp increase in oil prices charged by OPEC since 1973 may have helped to reduce Soviet influence in the Middle East and to increase the risks for Soviet foreign policy in the area.[17] As the OPEC states have become wealthier, they have turned to the West for machinery, arms, and technicians, now available for hard currency; the Western states, whatever their fears about shipping arms to the Middle East, have welcomed such sales as a way to redress their balance of payments. Iran and Saudi Arabia, having acquired ever more sophisticated weapons from the West, are becoming more important counters to Soviet power. Ever more concerned to prevent another oil embargo, the United States has tilted more toward the Arab side in order to achieve a settlement of Arab-Israeli differences and prevent another Middle East war. Washington has also strengthened its naval presence in the Indian Ocean so as to counter any Soviet threat to international shipping lanes. Finally, as members of OPEC observe the manner in which Moscow has applauded their embargos and price hikes but undercut them by selective selling in the West, they must become more doubtful of the sincerity of Soviet support. In short, we see another instance of an exploitative policy generating short-term gains but tending in the long run to boomerang.

While stressing its magnanimity in buying foreign oil and gas from Northern Africa and Middle Eastern countries, Moscow has paid less for these products than it would have cost to produce them in

[16] Ibid., p. 227.
[17] Ibid., pp. 177–81.

Western Siberia; it has thus been possible to keep more Soviet resources in the ground while waiting for other developments to make Siberian fields more cost effective. Moscow has also saved on transportation costs when transferring oil from the Middle East or Africa to Cuban or Asian clients rather than shipping Soviet products from Black Sea ports. All this is in keeping with Moscow's emerging neomercantilist philosophy.[18]

What the Iranian case shows is that economic interest can surmount the tendency—whether in Moscow or the West—to regard Third World resources as being necessarily an arena for zero-sum competition. The related pattern of Soviet oil and natural-gas arrangements with Iran and other countries along the southern perimeter of the Soviet Union indicates also an awareness that political cordiality and economic correctness may net greater benefits for Soviet interests than the military interventions, subversions, demands for economic concessions, and pressures for territorial adjustments of the years following World War II.

Are there more such opportunities for complementary cooperation? If so, will they be perceived and implemented?

There is a potential here that can be directed in several quite different directions. Soviet aid can remain basically bilateral, probably tending to reduce ties between Third World countries and the West. If Third World ties with Moscow thicken, they can remain cordial and correct or serve as the foundation for Soviet penetration. Alternatively, developing countries may work out acceptable arrangements with both Moscow and the West; such arrangements may, on the model of Iranian natural gas, serve to intensify multilateral cooperation.

If the oil problems of the Soviet Union become more acute, as several 1977 CIA reports anticipate, this could skew Soviet behavior toward a greater willingness to seek accommodations in the mutual advantage or, alternatively, a harder-line, *kto kovo* approach.

If countries of the West and the Third World succeed in cultivating relationships of interdependence helpful to both sides, this could put pressure on Moscow to withdraw from the field, join in global endeavors, or intensify its forward strategies.

Despite the potential for global cooperation, the political thrust behind Soviet policy is more likely to aim at undermining relations between the Third World and the West and turning the developing countries toward Moscow. Hence, a Soviet forward strategy is more

[18] Ibid., p. 117.

likely in the Third World than is globalist cooperation. Indeed, autarky is probably more likely than globalism.

Autarky?

If the Soviet leaders believe that their problems at home or in Eastern Europe are caused or aggravated by contacts with outsiders, they will probably try to limit such associations to the bare minimum judged necessary to sustain modernization of the Soviet economy and maintain Russia's image as a superpower. Demands for more autonomy by non–Great Russians and for greater liberalization will probably gain momentum in the Soviet Union and Eastern Europe for endogenous reasons, but some Kremlin officials will be tempted to make bourgeois influences a scapegoat for such difficulties, whatever their origin.

An inward orientation will be the more likely if Moscow, despite large economic outlays and some political risks, finds its overtures rebuffed or its influence shrinking in the Third World or the West.

But a radical pullback to isolationism is unlikely for several reasons. First, the historical pattern of tsarist as well as Soviet foreign policy has been to probe almost incessantly for targets of opportunity along Russia's periphery. If Moscow's advances stall in the West, they have usually continued in the East or the South (or both). Now that the Soviet Union commands the global reach of a superpower, extending to the high seas as well as the depths of outer space, a return to some kind of Fortress Russia posture is almost unthinkable. It would vitiate Communist ideology as well as Soviet power interests. The world outside the Soviet sphere is far from monolithic, moreover, and cracks and fissures will continually appear, tempting Soviet intervention. At the same time, despite Russia's relative self-sufficiency, Moscow will find pressing compulsions to seek solutions to its own economic and environmental problems in international programs.

As noted in the preceding chapter, there is also the web of material interest generating a substantial stake for expanding circles of Soviet leaders and other citizens in enhanced ties with the outside world. The privileges of the new "new class" and those who aspire to its ranks can hardly be achieved by autarky.

The prospects of some hermetically sealed, neo-Byzantine empire are equally dim. Great Russians, like others, may articulate their utopian dreams, but Moscow already has more than it can do to maintain its present levels of control over Eastern Europe. The nationalist resistance of East Europeans to Soviet domination probably exceeds the lust of Russian nationalists for hegemony. As energy shortages intensify, Moscow urges the East Europeans to reduce their dependence on the Soviet Union for resources. As countries of CEMA develop greater ties with the West and the Third World, Moscow's leverage will decrease.

Neither a Fortress Russia nor a closed neo-Byzantine empire is really feasible for the Soviet Union in the decades ahead. Indeed, neither extreme—globalism or autarky—is likely to predominate in Soviet policy.

Forward Strategy?

The Soviet Union is likely to continue or even heighten its campaign to turn the Third World from the West (or China) toward the Soviet camp if these efforts seem to yield a solid return. Though the Soviet Union needs relatively few of the Third World's mineral resources, it would like to be able to deprive the West of them. Soviet strategists would doubtless like to oust Western military rivals from bases in the Third World and obtain secure bases for their own naval and other foreign operations. As China grows in military and political stature, the Kremlin will want to secure allies to contain Peking's influence in the Third World. If the domestic and external policies of Third World nations paid greater obeisance to Soviet leadership, this would also strengthen the legitimacy and élan of Soviet Communism.

But Moscow will probably keep its campaigns in the Third World below the threshold where they could seriously jeopardize détente and trade with the West. History and bitter experience suggest that revolutionary movements in the Third World are unstable and undependable.[19] Today's victor may be the victim of tomorrow's coup. Even if the beneficiary of Soviet largess remains in power, he may decide to return to the embrace of the former colonial power (where he may have been educated and may have acquired some Western tastes). Why then should Moscow risk good relations with Washington for the sake of a Pyrrhic victory in the Third World? A Soviet foothold in South Africa or Brazil might justify a major effort, but Washington would more likely mount a large counteroffensive there than in Angola or even Peru.

If it is feasible for Third World suppliers of raw materials or other goods to obtain higher prices from Western markets, they are likely to seek improved terms of trade regardless of Soviet encourage-

[19] For an account of Moscow's increasing difficulties in Egypt, Libya, Somalia, Ethiopia, and other portions of Africa, see Joseph C. Harsch, "Grip on Upper Africa: Soviets' Sand Castle," *Christian Science Monitor*, July 29, 1977, p. 26.

ment. Moscow has few lessons to teach OPEC or the bauxite or coffee cartels of this world. Why should the Kremlin risk the wrath of the West for actions that may be taken by the Third World independent of Soviet policies?

The calculus of gain and loss also suggests that the difficulties of others do not necessarily redound to the advantage of Russia. The Soviet camp may not be profoundly vulnerable to economic dislocations abroad, but it is certainly sensitive. Inflation triggered by higher energy costs has increased the prices which countries of CEMA must pay for foreign products and reduced outside demand for goods from the East. Whatever the short-term gains Moscow might extract from Western vulnerability to suppliers in the Third World, the countries of CEMA find themselves locked into long-term patterns of partial interdependence with the West. What hurts the West can and has hurt CEMA on the rebound.

Détente and Trade?

Brezhnev's successors are likely to continue his interest in improving relations with the West if this orientation promises a substantial contribution to preventing a major war, reducing the economic burden of the arms race, modernizing the Soviet economy, and preventing American policies that could unleash China against the Soviet Union.

The incentives to Moscow to pursue détente and trade with the West will be multiplied if the Western nations appear capable of resolving their own internal and foreign problems. Western prosperity and scientific and technological progress serve as a magnet to the East, particularly when the countries of CEMA flounder in their own efforts at integration and at narrowing the gaps in their own living standards and technical prowess in relation to those of the West.

While the orientation toward détente and trade is most likely to predominate, we should also note the many factors that could unsettle this course. If Western nations wallow in their own economic and political crises so that contradictions within and among them seem ever more acute, Moscow could be tempted to step up its anti-Western campaigns in the Third World and to foment chaos in the enemy's home ground. Southern Europe—from Turkey to Portugal—has appeared particularly unstable in recent years, but Soviet observers also follow with great interest the persistent social and economic malaise of the United Kingdom and other countries of northern Europe and North America.

A root dilemma for the Kremlin leadership is the contradiction between optimal conditions for Soviet external and internal security. If the costs to the stability of Soviet rule in the Soviet Union and the influence of Moscow in Eastern Europe are high, the gains from arms negotiations and various exchange programs could appear exorbitantly expensive.

The objective reality is that the Soviet Union is theoretically the country least vulnerable to shortages of material resources. But the Soviet Union is probably more threatened than any other country by hostile neighbors, many heavily armed and dissatisfied with the boundaries, ideology, and political controls dictated by Moscow. The Kremlin also sees itself challenged domestically by dissident and ethnic political and ethnic forces egged on by outsiders. The world's giant fears that it stands on feet of clay. "What would happen if Soviet dissenters were simply permitted to voice their opinions without government interference?" a Soviet Embassy official in Washington was asked early in 1977. He replied, "Our society would fall apart."

Both the United States and the Soviet Union are hostage to one another strategically, but the Soviet Union is vulnerable domestically to Western influences without possessing a corresponding wedge by which the values and power systems of American society could be threatened. This leaves a major asymmetry in the correlation of forces. Soviet and East European citizens are eager for radio programs, films, books, and goods from the West; few Westerners display comparable interest in things Soviet. The economic and other problems of some Western countries have been severe and may grow even more acute, but Moscow has had little or no responsibility for inducing these crises, and few Westerners look to the Soviet Union for an answer to them. Even the Communist parties of Italy and France may prove, on balance, more threatening to Soviet-style institutions in Eastern Europe than to traditional democratic values in the West. Portugal, to take another example, has replaced right-wing dictatorship with democratic socialism rather than Soviet socialism.

Herein lies a Soviet weakness potentially more troublesome for the Kremlin than its technological backwardness in comparison with the West. The propagandists of the Kremlin can trumpet the virtues of a Soviet life style and socialist civilization, but they run up against the stubborn reality that many Soviet citizens and most East Europeans look westward for spiritual nourishment as well as material advances.

Whether or not Moscow collaborates in East-West or North-South endeavors, it may find that bourgeois values become stronger at home, in Eastern Europe, and in the Third World. Can the Soviet life style hope to compete with the more affluent standards and freedom of choice associated with the West? If the orientation toward détente and trade prevails and achieves its immediate objectives, the Kremlin may be faced with spirals of rising expectations very difficult to gratify in the framework of a work-oriented, authoritarian system. To all these challenges Brezhnev's successors might respond by trying to batten down the hatches.

We cannot be sure at what point Kremlin sensitivities may flare over these issues. Moscow paused before intervening in 1968 against Western-style socialism in Czechoslovakia; it sought to placate U.S. demands for more Jewish emigration in 1972–1973, only to pull back when Americans raised the ante.[20] The West has some leverage in these matters, but it is limited. While the Kremlin may make some compromises in order to minimize its strategic vulnerability and overcome its economic weaknesses, it will be much more rigid on matters affecting domestic security.

Since the prime concern of the Soviet leaders is the security of their own regime, they cannot be expected to bow to demands for human rights which they believe threaten that security or to join in globalist undertakings appearing irrelevant if not counter to fundamental interests at home.

Brezhnev's successors will argue whether détente and trade with the West offer substantial or merely marginal contributions to the alleviation of Russia's problems. Are the atmospherics of détente really necessary to prevent nuclear war? Are not Moscow's missiles the main deterrent? Have arms negotiations led to any diminution of the arms race? Has détente really opened the door to a free flow of technology and trade with the West? Will not some Western businessmen sell whatever they can to the East regardless of the political atmosphere? Will not China be dissuaded from adventurous policies by the same kind of military force that keeps the West at bay?

Such questions become more pressing if the orientation toward détente and trade compels the Soviet Union to forgo significant oppor-

---

[20] From 1948 through 1969, approximately 7,600 Soviet Jews emigrated to Israel. After 1970, emigration to Israel increased dramatically. Since 1973, however, that emigration has fallen off. The following approximate figures indicate the numbers of Soviet exit visas for Israel issued to Soviet citizens: 1970, 1,000; 1971, 14,000; 1972, 31,500; 1973, 33,500; 1974, 20,000; 1975, 13,000; 1976, 14,000. The Jewish emigration rate in early 1977 was about the same as it was in 1976. The number of Soviet exit visas for the United States issued to Jews has remained stable, ranging from about 500 in 1973 to 650 in 1976. (Statistics made available by U.S. Department of State, Bureau of Public Affairs, July 1977.)

tunities in the Third World or to jeopardize the internal security of the socialist camp.

If negotiations with the West enhance the external security of the Kremlin without adding greatly to internal tensions in Eastern Europe or the Soviet Union, the orientation toward détente could be justified on its own terms. In that case, it would be less painful for Moscow to pass up targets of opportunity in the West or the Third World if exploiting them meant risking the whole structure of détente and trade. Such sacrifices would be still less onerous if Moscow considered revolutionary advances in such areas not worth the price or if the Kremlin could persuade progressive forces throughout the world that détente served their interests as well as the interest of Moscow.

Mixed Model?

Soviet leaders, like those elsewhere, are likely to be pulled in different directions by incompatible objectives, both at home and abroad, and

TABLE 2

WHAT THE SOVIET UNION STANDS TO GAIN AND LOSE FROM DETENTE AND TRADE OR GLOBALISM

Probable Gains

External security: greater probability of East-West peace and arms control

Economics: greater prospects for trade, credits, and access to Western technology; some leverage on Western policy through interested economic groups

Domestic security: enhancing appeal of the regime by successes of peace program and higher standards of living

Ideology: keeping Marxism-Leninism in tune with changing realities

Probable Losses

Domestic security: pollution of elites and masses by bourgeois values and Western influences

Eastern Europe: disruption of Soviet influences and controls

Economics: acquisition of earlier generations of Western technology at high cost; delay in fundamental reforms needed for self-sustaining growth

Third World: probable strengthening of Western influence and decline in perceived need for association with Soviet camp against imperialism

by the difficulty of tailoring goals to means. This problem is underscored in Table 2, which suggests the way in which an adviser to the Politburo might draw up an interdependence/security balance sheet.

The priority of world peace and the imperatives of economic modernization are likely to keep the Kremlin on the track toward détente and trade with the West; temptations to exploit weaknesses in the Third World, combined with the slow growth of an expansionist warrior class, are likely to evoke forward strategies in the Third World, but below the threshold judged tolerable for détente between East and West; Soviet officials will also try to insulate their people from pollution by bourgeois values and to husband the natural resources of the Soviet Union.

Over the long haul—say through the late 1980s or 1990s—Soviet participation in globalist endeavors becomes more and more likely, partly because the Soviet Union—by then more open and probably more efficient—will be better able to take part in multilateral activities and partly because of momentum: limited interdependence with the West may snowball toward interdependence between North and South as well.

This assessment reflects an underlying pessimism about the prospects for self-sustaining growth in the Soviet system as it is now constituted; guarded optimism about the long-term prospects of the Soviet Union, on the basis of its vast resources and the renaissance of critical and humanistic thinking that has taken place there in recent decades; and a somewhat deeper confidence that reason, innovation, and good will will help the human race to survive and flourish rather than succumb to ecological or military catastrophes.

5

Policy Implications for the West

Modern life changes no longer century by century, but year by year, ten times faster than it ever has before—populations doubling, civilizations unified more closely with other civilizations, economic interdependence, racial questions, and—we're dawdling along. My idea is that we've got to go very much faster.

F. Scott Fitzgerald, 1920

It is important to realize that science exchange is not a zero-sum game. Thus, the goal of negotiations should be to obtain more *information, not to give less.*

National Academy of Sciences, 1977

As Americans, we cannot overlook the way our fate is bound with that of other nations. This interdependence stretches from the health of our economy to the security of our energy supplies. It is a new world, in which we cannot afford to be narrow in our vision, limited in our foresight, or selfish in our purpose. . . .

We want to see the Soviets further engaged in the growing pattern of international activities designed to deal with human problems—not only because they can be of real help, but also because we both should have a greater stake in the creation of a constructive and peaceful world order.

President Jimmy Carter, 1977

U.S. and Soviet Evolution: Toward Interdependence?

If Moscow's recognition of the principles of interdependence is compared with Washington's, a wavering but growing commitment is seen in both capitals. Each would prefer to avoid dependence upon resources from abroad, to eschew entangling alliances or détentes, and to be beyond reach of have-nots crying or threatening retaliation. But even superpowers seem unable to free themselves from external ties that bind.

Both the United States and the Soviet Union have come a long

F. Scott Fitzgerald, *This Side of Paradise* (New York: Scribners, 1970), p. 272.

way from the isolationist thinking that characterized their policies for decades. Americans have come further, in part, because they had further to go. Though dependent upon foreign investment and to some degree upon the protection of the British Navy in the nineteenth century, Americans tended to credit their economic well-being and freedom from foreign wars to divine blessings and their own determined enterprise. When Americans became creditors to the world during the First World War they quickly assumed this to be the natural order. Even the whiplash effects of the Great Depression did little to jar Americans' awareness of the common fate of mankind, and they sought to remain neutral despite the growing war dangers in Europe and Asia.

The United States tried returning to Fortress America in 1945–1946, only to feel compelled to fill breaches from Turkey to Germany to Korea and later to Vietnam. Following the Truman Doctrine and America's entry into the field of developmental assistance, many U.S. citizens adjusted to the idea that others depended on them, but they were slow to consider accepting American dependence upon others. Thus, the initial reaction of Presidents Nixon and Ford to the economic and energy crises of the early 1970s was to shake U.S. financial and trade relations loose from existing international accords (manufactured in the U.S.A.), and to base the energy policies of the country upon a Project Independence. Only under duress did they espouse (concurrently) a Project Interdependence. The "trilateralist" assumptions of the Carter administration are more conducive to globalist approaches, but it too wishes to limit resource dependence to the extent feasible within existing economic, technological, and political parameters.[1]

Russians, at least since Peter the Great, have been profoundly conscious of their dependency upon foreign trade and transfer of technology. In the decades before World War I the tsars permitted and encouraged Russia's industrialization to be financed and managed largely by foreigners. Though the Soviet regime expropriated foreign interests, the Bolsheviks negotiated mining concessions in the 1920s and set about acquiring mass production techniques and modern technology from the West in much the same spirit as Peter had.

In the interwar years, as in the 1970s, the Kremlin admitted that the U.S.S.R. was becoming more closely entwined with the capitalist world, but asserted that the socialist fatherland was beyond the reach

[1] See also Trilateral Commission Task Force report no. 13, *Collaboration with Communist Countries in Managing Global Problems: An Examination of the Options*, (New York: The Trilateral Commission, 1977).

of the spasmodic ups and downs of Western business cycles.[2] Anticipating the position that Rumania has taken toward CEMA, the 1927 CPSU Congress asserted that the Soviet Union did not intend to strengthen the existing international division of labor or become an agrarian appendage of the capitalist economic system.[3] Still, when the Great Depression struck, Stalin's Russia found few markets or new creditors abroad.

In the 1930s the Soviet leaders also recognized an interdependency in the security realm. Behind Litvinov's slogan "peace is indivisible," the Soviet Union became the staunchest supporter of collective security in the League of Nations. Though not so fetishistic about international organization as President Roosevelt, Stalin probably would have preferred a continuation of the wartime alliance in the United Nations to its degeneration into cold war rivalry.

The Soviet Union imported more goods from the United States than from any other country in 1923–1924, 1924–1925, 1930, 1935, 1937, 1938, 1939, and 1940, the peak year being 1930, when these imports reached about $230 million. Utilizing lend-lease credits, the Soviet Union was the largest purchaser of U.S. goods in 1946—roughly $236 million. By 1950, however, Soviet imports from the United States had declined to less than $10 million a year.[4]

Stalin's most autarkic act was to cut off the Soviet Union and its East European satellites from participation in the European Recovery Program (Marshall Plan). This action reinforced and deepened the political cleavage between East and West. As the West adopted trade restrictions on strategic goods exported to the Soviet Union, a vicious circle emerged separating both sides economically and politically.

If the Soviet Union could survive autarkically in the 1930s, it could get by much more easily in the post–World War II era, when its neighbors could be enlisted to support Soviet economic development. CEMA, founded in January 1949, was used at least until the mid-1950s as a vehicle for Soviet exploitation of the East European

---

[2] G. Zinoviev, "The Partial 'Stabilization' of Capitalism and the Tasks of the Comintern and the Russian Communist Party (Bolshevik)," *Kommunisticheskii Internatsional*, no. 5 (May 1925), pp. 5–47 at p. 27. Earlier in the year Karl Radek asserted that differences among capitalist countries made it possible to predict that Soviet exports would be able to break through the financial blockade erected to keep them from Western markets: "Results of the 'Era of Democracy and Pacifism'," *Kommunisticheskii Internatsional*, no. 2 (February 1925), pp. 77–93.

[3] Cited by Daniel Yergin in "Politics and Soviet-American Trade: The Three Questions," *Foreign Affairs*, vol. 55, no. 3 (April 1977), pp. 517–38 at p. 520.

[4] Germany and Britain were the other leading exporters to the Soviet Union. Marshall I. Goldman, *Détente and Dollars* (New York: Basic Books, 1975), pp. 14–15, 21.

economies. By 1950 more than 80 percent of total Soviet exports and imports were confined to East Europe and China.

The extent of change in recent years is suggested by Marshall Goldman's remark that Brezhnev came to the United States in 1973 stressing that he had come not to bury, but to buy. This was in sharp contrast to the attitude shown in 1959, when Khrushchev boasted that the Soviet Union would overtake and surpass U.S. economic output by 1970 or 1980 at the latest.

> Who would have dreamed back in 1959 that one day the Chase Manhattan Bank would open an office at 1 Karl Marx Square, or that the chairman of the New York Stock Exchange and the national commander of the American Legion would go to Moscow as honored guests?

Until 1971 American exports to the Soviet Union rarely amounted to more than $100 million a year, but they jumped to $550 million in 1972. American exports to the Soviet Union totaled $1.19 billion in 1973, buoyed by the wheat deal, but fell to half that level in 1974.[5]

In some respects—both military-strategic and economic—the Soviet Union has shown a greater dedication to acceptance of interdependence between East and West than has the United States. Though each side made important concessions to reach the 1972 SALT accords and the 1974 Vladivostok understanding, Moscow probably gave up even more than Washington did: limiting ABM in the face of present danger from China (quite remote for the United States); in effect not counting the forward-based systems of the United States and the independent and shared nuclear forces of other NATO powers; ignoring for the nonce the more than five-year lead of the United States in MIRV deployment. To judge from the wide support garnered by the Jackson critique of SALT I, it seems unlikely that Congress would ever have approved analogous sacrifices by the United States. Judging by the congressional response in 1977 to the nomination of Paul Warnke as head of U.S. Arms Control and Disarmament Agency and chief SALT negotiator, and by the persistent appeal of "Panel B"-type alarums, the "present danger" school remains determined to resist any such sacrifices in the future.[6]

---

[5] Ibid., pp. 1–2; additional data concerning trade are given below in the section "Two Perspectives."

[6] Among others, Richard Pipes, "Why the Soviet Union Thinks It Could Fight and Win a Nuclear War," *Commentary*, vol. 64, no. 4 (July 1977), pp. 21–34. For a rebuttal, see Walter C. Clemens, Jr., "The 'Dangerists': Whipping the Arms Race," *Newsday*, January 9, 1978; also Warnke's January 19, 1978 press conference on SALT, the transcript of which shows that several editors, earlier suspicious of him, expressed respect for his "knowledge" and "evident wisdom."

Though Brezhnev has doubtless been challenged by voices recommending that the Soviet Union remain aloof from the chaotic conjunctures of world capitalism, he has committed the country to long-term deals, such as those worked out with Occidental Petroleum to fructify over twenty years, and to large-scale programs involving the presence of hundreds of foreign technicians on Soviet soil and many Soviet technicians in training programs abroad.[7] Many Westerners, meanwhile, continue to see trade as aid to the Soviet Union and seek to keep Western credits at a low level and to maintain a long list of embargoed goods. While the White House may think in non-zero-sum terms, many congressmen and powerful interest groups still regard East-West relations as a struggle in which one side or the other must prevail. Many welcome the demands of Jewish dissidents and others within the Soviet Union as an excuse for making East-West trade contingent upon quite unlikely changes in Soviet domestic policy.

And while Moscow officially refuses to permit Western interference in its domestic affairs (human rights, and so forth), even here it has trod lightly and made some concessions (on emigration and the treatment of some dissidents) to Western preferences—a remarkable shift considering the traditions of tsarist as well as of Soviet rule.

John P. Hardt and George D. Holliday have found that Soviet political authorities and economic planners have moved far from their interwar insistence that technological transfers leave the Soviet Union independent of the Western supplier. Rather, companies such as Fiat and Swindell-Dressler are encouraged by Soviet authorities

> to expect long-term, expanding relations. Moreover, the policy of the earlier period of producing a Soviet plant in the indigenous administrative setting has been . . . modified. There appears to be increasing acceptance of the ideal that

---

[7] Arguing that "vast prospects are open as a result of the development" of Soviet-American cooperation, Dr. Gvishiani, in the speech cited earlier, recalled Brezhnev's words to a delegation of American businessmen: "The U.S.S.R. and the U.S.A. are the countries of biggest economic potential. Rich natural resources are at our disposal. We frankly admit that you, the Americans, are ahead of us in some fields. But, in other fields, we are ahead. So, if we make a joint effort and take a broad, far-reaching approach with a long-term view, say, some twenty-year projections, we shall become aware of the fact that vast possibilities are being opened." (*Pravda*, June 24, 1973.)

Gvishiani asserted that "the most important feature of the contemporary stage in the development of economic relations between the U.S.S.R. and the most advanced countries in Western Europe and also Japan and Canada is passing over from sporadic commercial deals, to a *planned and programmed economic cooperation on a stable and long-term basis.* One can hardly underestimate both the economic and social implications of this tendency." (Emphasis added.)

> improved performance requires not only broad Western involvement in the entire cycle of technology transfer, but also new kinds of production facilities that more fully adapt Western managerial and technical experiences to Soviet conditions.

What Hardt and Holliday term the "modified systems approach, especially through joint management, and production decisions" may, they believe, make the Soviet system as a whole more open to Western influences.[8]

There has been, in short, a rapid evolution since the Stalin years when national sovereignty and noninterference in domestic affairs dominated Soviet thinking about relations with the outside world. While zero-sum thinking persists in Moscow, more pervasively than in Washington, the Politburo centrists seem to have adopted a variable-sum or even positive-sum orientation toward strategic and economic problems with the West; the full rigors of their *kto kovo* Leninist assumptions are reserved for the Chinese, for competitions in the Third World, and for those Soviet citizens who openly doubt the sagacity of CPSU rule. Toward the West, however, Khrushchev's formulation still holds sway in Moscow: "Peaceful coexistence and cooperation are dictated by life itself."

What we may be witnessing in the 1970s is a gradual transition in which the Kremlin accepts relationships with the West which make the Soviet Union not just "sensitive" to external events but which would be highly disruptive for Soviet economic and technological development if severed. Such relationships do not make Soviet material well-being contingent on externals in the way that Japan depends on oil, but they are moving along the spectrum from mere sensitivity toward deep vulnerability. At home the Kremlin probably exaggerates the degree to which internal dissidence leaves the Soviet state sensitive or even vulnerable to external manipulation, but even its response to this problem is colored by knowledge that external security is absolutely dependent on avoiding nuclear war.

Soviet and Western Priorities

Western analysts and policy makers are confronted with manifold uncertainties. How serious are the energy, food, and other crises that

[8] John P. Hardt and George D. Holliday, "Technology Transfer and Change in the Soviet Economic System" (Paper prepared for a conference on Technology and Communist Culture, Villa Serbelloni, Bellagio, Italy, revised December 1976).

impel thoughtful persons all over the world to speak of interdependence? How feasible are cooperative solutions? How wide-ranging must such cooperation be in order to achieve its objectives?

Uncertainties mount as we seek to understand the extent to which Soviet policy makers judge cooperative programs to be feasible or useful for their interests. A philosopher would probably counsel outsiders to resign themselves to agnosticism. We simply do not know the deepest meanings behind the words and deeds from which we seek to infer the intentions and expectations of Soviet leaders. The outsider has little sure knowledge about the makeup and relative strengths of competing tendencies in Soviet politics; he must interpret trends in official Soviet publications and other media without knowing what debates and struggles take place behind the scenes and in the corridors of the Kremlin; he does not know what thresholds may determine Soviet tolerance of domestic unrest or other challenges to Kremlin interests that might be attributed to external influences.

Notwithstanding these uncertainties, statesmen must act. To act wisely, they must plan. In Table 3 I attempt to rank the relative likelihood of alternative Soviet strategies for the next one to two decades (as argued in the preceding chapter) and the relative utility of these approaches, given the values of most Western countries. (These values, I believe, correspond to those of most Soviet liberals and probably to the interests of most of humanity.) If this ordering is correct, the problem for Western policy makers is how to organize globalist programs so that they can go forward, lacking Soviet participation but without driving the Kremlin away from détente and trade and toward an unsettling forward strategy.

TABLE 3

RELATIVE PROBABILITY OF ALTERNATIVE SOVIET STRATEGIES AND THEIR UTILITY FOR THE WEST (LATE 1970S THROUGH 1980S)

Probability	*Utility*
1. Mixed Model	1. Globalism
2. Détente and Trade	2. Détente and Trade
3. Forward Strategy	3. Autarky
4. Autarky	4. Mixed Model
5. Globalism	5. Forward Strategy

Two Perspectives: Dangers and Opportunities in Closer East-West Ties

How far and in what ways should East-West relations be developed? Should Washington be concerned more with sustaining détente and preventing war, say, through 1984 or with a longer-range strategy looking toward 2000 and beyond? Should Washington endeavor to strengthen specific coalitions and interest groups and coalitions within the Soviet Union or assume that such manipulation is beyond its ken or ability? Is it in the interest of the West to help liberalizing forces within the Soviet Union, even if by modernizing the system we—and they—help to create a more vigorous economic rival to the United States and Western Europe?

Even if we assume that, in principle, more commercial, technological, and scientific ties with the Soviet Union are desirable, a series of difficult questions remains:

- How can East-West trade be made a two-way flow? How can Western markets for CEMA be generated so CEMA countries can better pay for imports from the West? Would this task be substantially aided if Washington granted most-favored-nation treatment to all CEMA states?
- What mechanisms for credits are most useful? On what terms should credit be extended? What limits should be imposed on CEMA levels of indebtedness to the West?
- What limits should be imposed on the sale of advanced Western technology to the East—and by what means? How can the West ensure that scientific and technological exchange programs are not a one-way street?
- How much grain or other commodities should be sold to the Soviet Union if this raises prices for Western consumers or prevents the West and countries of the Third World from establishing adequate food reserve systems?
- To what extent should the West facilitate Soviet participation in multinational institutions and projects if this gives Moscow more leverage to sabotage them from within?

To what degree should politics govern? Should Western governments make changes in their trade and exchange policies contingent upon changes in Soviet policies—at home or abroad? And if considerations of political linkage are to predominate, should they be pessimistic or optimistic? Cautious about the prospects of dealing with a totalitarian, authoritarian superpower? Or confident about the prospects of working out accommodations to mutual advantage? Should we take risks for peace or presume, with Laertes, that "best safety lies in fear"?

Though Western analysts give a variety of cross-cutting answers to these questions, two basic perspectives have emerged. The more cautious approach advises: Let sleeping giants lie. Let us keep all exchanges with the U.S.S.R. to a minimum.[9] Even if Moscow does not exploit such exchanges to enhance its military posture, there is no point in building up the Soviet state into a true economic superpower by improving its technological base and management techniques; by granting it long-term credits sometimes tantamount to aid; by facilitating its capacity to wreck the delicately balanced mechanisms of interdependence worked out between like-minded governments in the free world. We should not permit East-bloc debts to rise so that Western creditors become anxious. If we are to have more dealings with the U.S.S.R., let them be conditioned on deeds—not mere words—showing that the Soviet system has become more humane and ready to live in peace. Until that time, let them live in a Fortress Russia or sealed neo-Byzantine empire, choking on the intrinsic inefficiencies of their authoritarian regime. If they act aggressively abroad, we must step up our own capacity and willingness to rebuff all Soviet expansionism. While we would like to help the plight of Soviet citizens, this is beyond our capacity. It would be dangerous—for their security and ours—to encourage any belief that we stand by ready to assist reformist elements within the Soviet realm.

The more optimistic orientation calls—not for the erection of a wall around the Soviet realm—but for a steady effort to reduce the barriers impeding trade in ideas and goods between the East and the West. The optimistic believes that it is undesirable and virtually infeasible to calculate, Scrooge-like, the gains and losses in East-West exchanges. In the words of a study by the National Academy of Sciences, "it is important to realize that science exchange is *not* a zero-sum game. Thus, the goal of negotiations should be to obtain

[9] That a new kind of technology implantation is afoot—throughout the world—threatening to undermine U.S. interests is argued by Jack Baranson in "Technology Exports Can Hurt Us," *Foreign Policy*, no. 25 (Winter 1976–77), pp. 180–94. Another form of technology transfer—potentially much more dangerous—plutonium spread, is discussed in the same issue by Albert Wohlstetter, "Spreading the Bomb without Quite Breaking the Rules," pp. 88–96, 145–79.

more information, not to give *less*."[10] Applied to business or security transactions, this approach suggests that the aim should be mutual enrichment—not one-sided gain.[11] If either side seeks unilateral gains at the expense of the other, not many agreements will be concluded; those that are signed will not endure. Businessmen, it is assumed, will determine from their own profit-and-loss statements whether their particular enterprises gain sufficiently from East-West trade to justify their perseverance.

The optimist has not forgotten that there is a potential for conflict as well as for mutual advantage in East-West relations. He believes it is necessary to be on guard against the possibility that the other side may seek to exploit the relationship for one-sided gain. But he does not convert this caution into a self-fulfilling prophecy. If we act on the premise that every Soviet gesture of good will contains a secret weapon, we will give Moscow little incentive to negotiate and act in good faith. Our ultradefensive posture may generate the very dangers it was calculated to repress.[12] At a minimum this approach inhibits our seeking and weighing opportunities for cooperation that might have merit on their own terms.[13]

One of the most thoughtful proponents of caution in expanding economic ties with the Soviet Union has been Gregory Grossman. He notes that though Moscow has displayed a gargantuan appetite for Western goods and capital since the 1920s, it has been unwilling to change its political spots, internally or externally.

> On the contrary, the more successful the Soviet regime is in obtaining Western economic co-operation without any significant political quid-pro-quos, the more freedom of action is it likely to sense in both domestic and foreign spheres.

---

[10] "Findings and Recommendations," *Review of US/USSR Agreement on Cooperation in the Fields of Science and Technology*, p. 86.

[11] Problems in reciprocation have been analyzed in Edward A. Hewett, "On Most-Favored Nation Agreements Between Market and Centrally Planned Economies" (Paper presented at the Kennan Institute, February 23–25, 1977).

[12] This was the fate, for example, of efforts by France to suppress Germany within the one-sided framework of the Versailles system.

[13] Thus, an otherwise well-balanced and comprehensive study by the Congressional Reference Service contains many pages about America's interdependence with the Third World, but presents the Soviet Union solely as an antagonist, with no discussion of a possible overlap of U.S. and Soviet interests. Is this because senior researchers of the Library of Congress want to avoid any impression of being soft on communism? Or have they simply internalized the zero-sum assumptions of the Cold War era and kept them pristine? Whatever the explanation, such studies restrict Washington horizons needlessly by failing to analyze alternatives to East-West conflict. See, for example, *The Soviet Union and The Third World: A Watershed in Great Power Policy?*, p. 174.

> The notion that the Soviets will by means of economic ties become "enmeshed in a web of mutual economic interdependence" is conjectural at best. As we have noticed, they take the proffered benefits and are careful to avoid those steps that would "enmesh" them or change their wonted ways. As a result, "mutual interdependence" can easily turn into *double* dependence on our part: we could become dependent on their good will in repaying debts and shipping key materials such as energy, and at the same time also on their market for goods of interest to strong pressure groups in this country.[14]

Such warnings are well taken, but the historical record shows that the Soviet regime has a good record of observing its commercial undertakings. Deviation from this procedure would undermine the image which Moscow had long labored to promote among the financiers and traders of the capitalist world. To be sure, Moscow sometimes exploits legal loopholes so as to bend the spirit if not the letter of its obligations, for example, using European intermediaries in 1977 to purchase more U.S. grain than permitted without special authorization. But flagrant abuse of economic obligations to the West would undermine the entire structure and send détente into a tailspin. Surely the Western governments will not permit themselves to become so dependent upon Soviet supplies of energy or other key resources that they could be vulnerable to Soviet *diktat*. Pressure groups within the United States are an ever-present complication for U.S. foreign policy. The voices of farmers and others with a stake in Soviet trade will be partially checked or outweighed by those working in contrary directions.

Grossman also warns that once the Soviet regime feels secure in its receipt of economic benefits from the West, it will surely give short shrift to those at home seeking to emigrate or obtain basic human rights. "Moscow opened the door to Jewish emigration in 1969, not after the Nixon-Brezhnev meetings that launched détente but in expectation of it." Grossman warns against throwing away bargaining leverage by granting Moscow long-term credits before it starts liberalization moving.

While it is clear that Moscow intensifies domestic repression to counter what it fears to be the effects of East-West associations, the fact is that since 1953 there has been a secular trend toward greater liberalization and tolerance for dissent. Grossman's model seems to

---

[14] Statement prepared for hearings by the U.S. Congress, Commission on Security and Cooperation in Europe, January 1977, p. 6.

exclude the possibility of any momentum in reciprocity, based on mutual concessions *after* as well as *before* any major accord. Grossman also passes over the many times when the West has lost its bargaining leverage by waiting too long to close a deal while seeking to obtain maximum concessions from the other side.[15]

All kinds of dire futures resulting from increased contacts between East and West are thinkable. But a study of senior executives in U.S. firms dealing with the Soviet Union in the mid-1970s showed that the 74 percent (from 168 respondents) evaluated the experiences of their companies' in the Soviet market as profitable. Of the 9 percent reporting significant losses, most were firms inexperienced or poorly prepared for dealing with the Soviet system.[16]

Respondents indicated that most U.S. exports have been in the form of technology-as-product rather than licensed expertise. And the expertise transferred has tended to involve running a machine rather than making it. The qualitative sophistication of the technology transferred in the mid-1970s has probably been overstated in news reports. Though most respondents agreed that selling expertise rather than products to the Soviet Union would upgrade Soviet technology somewhat, most believe that fundamental weaknesses in the research and development cycle of the Soviet Union would prevent Russian research organizations from outstripping American capabilities.

U.S. firms have not suffered significantly from having to deal with Soviet foreign trade organizations despite Moscow's monopolistic potential to whiplash prospective vendors.[17] What does alienate many U.S. companies is the inordinate time required to conclude contracts with Soviet buyers and then to secure U.S. government approval. The relatively small volume of likely Russian purchases also reduces U.S. sales interest. The combination of these factors has led a U.S. executive to comment: "The Russians are cutting their own throats by the way they do business." Another added: "Who needs it?"

Apart from commercial transactions, a review of the various

---

[15] Walter C. Clemens, Jr., "When Diplomacy Dallies," *Christian Science Monitor*, November 22, 1977, p. 27.

[16] Other losers may have chosen not to respond. More than 400 firms were polled. See William F. Kolarik, Jr., "Executive Viewpoints on USA-USSR Commerce: A Preliminary Analysis," *International Studies Notes*, vol. 3, no. 4 (Winter 1976), pp. 22–27.

[17] As representatives of Occidental Petroleum and major grain exporters have told the present author, there are peculiarities in negotiating with representatives of any cultural system different from one's own. Negotiations with Japan, in their own way, require as much adaptability as those with the Soviet Union, if not more.

studies made to assess the pros and cons of East-West exchange programs suggests three reasons why it is almost impossible to calculate the pros and cons on the basis of the question, "Who has gained more?"[18]

First, outcomes cannot be compared when both sides are pursuing a variety of goals in different fields—political, economic, environmental, and so on. From the mid- or late-1950s to the present, the Soviet Union appears to have been primarily concerned with obtaining greater access to U.S. technology, while Americans have wanted to learn more about the Soviet social system. At the level of high politics, both Moscow and Washington have wanted to generate a network of trade and other relationships to make war less likely. We have, in short, an "apples and oranges" problem.

Second, even the more tangible objectives sought are difficult to measure. U.S. participants in exchanges of science and technology have difficulty assessing the net gains to either side from these programs. Neither U.S. nor (probably) Soviet specialists can measure what benefits redound to the Soviet economy from exposure to advanced Western technologies, because the foreign import may be skillfully or (more likely) clumsily assimilated. No one can measure the opportunity costs for the individuals and firms diverted from their regular occupations, nor compare the outcome of efforts at U.S.-Soviet cooperation, say, with more cooperation between the United States and Western Europe. Experts on Soviet science policy, for example, conclude that they have acquired little new factual information, but add that their feel for the subject matter has been enhanced. Most U.S. participants in the exchanges come away with a sense that there have been important intangible gains, virtually impossible to weigh next to the tangibles, even if the latter could be accurately assessed.

Third, one's assessment of the outcomes will vary sharply depending upon whether short- or long-term time horizons are used. If the criterion is "visible results in one to five years," one will necessarily exclude the gains made possible in the long run by improved communication, enhanced trust, concentration on projects most likely to be of joint interest, and institutional innovations geared to fit the needs of the exchange—in brief, the results of a steepened learning

[18] See, among others, Thomas and Kruse-Vaucienne, *Soviet Science and Technology*; Graham, "Speculative Analysis of the Soviet Perception of the S&T Agreement"; and Herbert Kupferberg, *The Raised Curtain: Report of the Twentieth Century Fund Task Force on Soviet-American Scholarly and Cultural Exchanges* (New York: Twentieth Century Fund, 1977).

curve when both sides are attempting to work out mutually rewarding projects in many domains for the first time in their checkered history.

The historian would hardly draw up a definitive balance sheet on East-West détente when it has been attempted for only a few years, and half-heartedly at that. Similarly, the fruits of commercial and other exchanges between East and West need time to ripen. Thus, the first comprehensive U.S.-Soviet educational and cultural exchange agreement signed in 1958 had the effect of centralizing all exchanges in government bureaucracies in Moscow and Washington, thereby institutionalizing many obstacles to the free exchanges between interested individuals and institutions on both sides. By the mid-1970s, however, bilateral agreements had been worked out between institutions of higher learning and major archives in both countries. It had taken almost two decades of frustrating trial and error, but the bureaucratic barricades were beginning to crumble.

While most transfer of technology so far has probably been from West to East, there has also been some flow in the other direction, with room for much wider exchange rather than unilateral transfer. The ways in which both sides can complement their efforts were illustrated on June 20, 1977, when the world's largest airplane, the U.S. C5-A, delivered at Moscow a 40-ton, $3.5 million magnet, constructed at the Argonne National Laboratory with support from ERDA. When cooled to 453 degrees below zero fahrenheit, the magnet enables either coal or gas to be converted into energy 50 percent more efficiently than before. Though the United States has excellent components, such as the magnet, the American program in magnetohydrodynamics has been cut back, while Moscow's has kept on. The U.S. magnet will be used at a Soviet plant with better testing facilities and more experience than exist in the United States. It is to be returned to the United States after two years.

U.S. participants in joint U.S.-Soviet scientific programs reported in 1976 that both sides have gained from exchanges, particularly in environmental protection programs. Americans have gained particularly from Soviet experience in prediction of earthquakes, seismological research, construction of high dams, and reduction of oil spills at sea.[19]

The flow of information and technology from East to West could probably be enhanced if Western needs and Soviet strengths were better known and communications improved. Soviets are being awarded hundreds of patents by the U.S. Patent Office and are con-

[19] See David K. Willis, "How Joint U.S.-Soviet Research Helps Both," *Christian Science Monitor*, November 18, 1976.

cluding licensing arrangements with U.S. firms to allow them to use Soviet technology. The chairman of the Control Data Corporation, William C. Norris, argues that there is a basis for a natural division of work, and cites examples, such as fusion research, where it has already profited both sides.[20]

The proponent of enhanced East-West ties agrees that it is difficult to measure outcomes from exchange programs, but he argues that each side can rank its objectives. Prevention of war between East and West, he contends, should stand at the top of the agenda. If economic or other transactions contribute just one part in the ten, or fifty, or a hundred factors reducing the likelihood of war, this contribution is probably more important than any gain or loss in other domains. Expanded trade cannot, by itself, be expected to prevent war, but it may make war less likely by providing incentives for stability, by laying the groundwork for expanded interaction, and by promoting communication.

After expanding at a rapid rate—total turnover in 1972–1974 was almost four times as great as that in 1969–1971—Soviet-U.S. trade leveled off in the mid-1970s after Moscow claimed that the Jackson-Vanik amendment on emigration and the Stevenson amendment on export credits violated the terms of the October 1972 U.S.-Soviet trade agreement.[21]

What are the feasible ways for Moscow to pay for imports? First, by export of raw materials, though domestic shortages—even in oil—may compete, and with gold; second, by exporting raw materials and semiprocessed goods resulting from the various projects—natural gas for pipelines, chemicals and fertilizers for chemical factories, and timber and coking coal in exchange for participation in development of Siberian timber and coal; a third possibility—exports of Soviet manufactured goods—seems to have become less attractive to Moscow because of difficulties in making Soviet products competitive in Western markets. But another kind of compensation agreement is illustrated in recent Bendix negotiations to help the Soviet Union establish a spark-plug factory and take a percentage of the output for marketing through its worldwide network.[22]

The current Five-Year Plan projects an increase of up to 35

---

[20] The CDC seeks to get a significant amount of "appropriate technology" (oriented toward needs of developing countries) and high technology into its TECH-OTEC data-base-sharing system to match needs of sellers and seekers all over the world. See William C. Norris, "Technological Cooperation for Survival" (Minneapolis: Control Data Corporation, February 1977).

[21] Yergin, "Politics and Soviet-American Trade: The Three Questions," p. 517.

[22] Ibid., p. 537.

percent in Soviet trade with the West. But economic and political interests on both sides will suffer if the Soviet Union cannot sell more goods in the West or work out new forms of compensation arrangements. If Moscow cannot earn more hard currency in trade, it may curtail imports, as it did in 1976, when imports rose only 4 percent throughout 1975; it may try to sell more arms to the Third World; or—if still higher levels of credit are extended—Moscow may gain more debtor leverage on the West.

Soviet exports increased 27 percent in 1976, but they still lagged imports, $14.8 billion to $9.9 billion. Soviet hard-currency debt rose from $2.5 billion in 1970 to $10 billion in 1975 to $14 billion in 1976 (all year-end figures). Other CEMA countries in 1974–1976 imported about 50 percent more from the West than they exported, making the 1976 balance $17.5 billion in imports to $11.3 billion in exports. Poland had the largest deficit in 1976, Rumania the least.[23]

The indebtedness of East European countries to the West leaves Western bankers sensitive but reflects a deepening dependency of most East European states upon the West.[24] If financial or economic ties were disrupted, they would suffer even more than would Western firms or financial institutions. If the flow of Western credits and technology were broken, this would be a serious setback for the East Europeans in their efforts to modernize and become competitive in international markets. If they cannot sell their products abroad, for example, how will they pay for oil? Having chosen to modernize through enhanced ties with the West, Poland and other members of CEMA find themselves increasingly dependent upon sustaining and intensifying those ties. Though Poland's trade with the West as a whole has in the 1970s steadily moved toward the overall level of Soviet-Polish trade, Warsaw is more vulnerable to a cutoff of supplies from the Soviet Union than from any single Western country. Poland and other East European regimes also remain dependent to some extent upon Moscow for *permission* to reform their economies, even though it may be difficult for them to modernize in deeper ways without more intensive reforms.[25]

While the proponent of East-West exchanges is hopeful, he also

---

[23] See Eugene Kozicharow, "Hard Currency Problems Spur Soviet Export Push," *Aviation Week and Space Technology*, April 11, 1977, p. 17; also Yergin, "Politics and Soviet-American Trade: The Three Questions," p. 535; also Sarah M. Terry, report on continuing research at U.S. Department of State, Bureau of External Research, June 23, 1977.

[24] If the West helps European countries work out their indebtedness, should this influence—or be made to influence—their dealings with Third World debtors?

[25] Terry, report on continuing research at U.S. Department of State, Bureau of External Research, June 23, 1977.

favors reasonable precautions. He would improve oversight committees established among OECD nations to identify and limit export of technologies and products likely to facilitate important improvements in Soviet military prowess.[26] He would set ceilings on the indebtedness of CEMA but would also seek ways to reduce it so that trade can flourish without undue East-bloc leverage with Western financial institutions.[27] Such caution is tempered, however, by awareness that the West leads in most important indexes of strategic, technological, and economic power. He knows that the Soviet Union is surrounded by hostile powers (including putative allies) and has much longer land and sea frontiers to defend than has any Western country, and thus has security requirements and traditions quite different from those of the United States.[28] While the Western countries are basically strong today, in the long run it will be important for all states—North and South, East and West—to improve their collaboration if they are to optimize the interests of their citizens in peace and security, economic well-being, environmental quality, and other elements of human development.[29]

To what extent is it feasible or desirable to attempt linkage in bargaining over economic, political, and other issues with Moscow? If linkage is based mainly on quid pro quo complementarity, this may well be in the interest of both sides. For example, the Yalta Conference gave Stalin what he wanted with respect to Poland, satisfied the United States with respect to the United Nations, and satisfied Britain with respect to France. If one side is the more eager for an agreement, it may offer more to achieve an accord than the other side may offer.

---

[26] Criteria are suggested by J. Fred Bucy in "On Strategic Technology Transfer to the Soviet Union," *International Security*, vol. 1, no. 4 (Spring 1977), pp. 25–43 at pp. 41–42.

[27] See the suggestions of Richard Portes, "East Europe's Debt to the West: Interdependence is a Two-Way Street," *Foreign Affairs*, vol. 55, no. 4 (July 1977), pp. 751–83 at pp. 777–82.

[28] See Walter C. Clemens, Jr., "America is Already 'Second to None'," *Washington Post*, November 15, 1976.

[29] But there is also a sense in which U.S. and Soviet citizens would gain if the rival superpower became more self-sufficient. This is a familiar idea in the realm of strategy: A secure second-strike deterrent enhances the security of both sides. But this may also be true in the economic realm. To the extent that either the United States or the Soviet Union can reduce its own imports, it reduces competition among other importers and increases competition among exporters. If the Soviet Union must import oil, this will raise the price of oil—not only for the OECD countries but for Moscow's partners in CEMA as well. If the Soviet Union must import grain, this benefits some American farmers but increases the price of grain (and meat)—not only for grain-importing countries but for U.S. consumers. *If* resources are finite, and if the giants consume less, more will be left for others.

Thus, the Khrushchev-Bulganin regime met Eisenhower's demand for "deeds, not words" by withdrawing from portions of Finland and Austria as the condition for the 1955 Geneva Summit. Another kind of linkage was suggested by Khrushchev in 1963: He would sign a nuclear test ban, but he wanted some sign of progress toward a NATO-Warsaw Pact security agreement. And his successors linked Vietnam and arms control: They initially spurned U.S. arms-control proposals while Washington was bombing a sister socialist state. Later, surprising most analysts, they agreed to some Jewish emigration as the price for improved trade conditions.

All this suggests that attempts to link one consideration with another are almost inevitable in international bargaining; indeed, Western governments may be almost compelled to do so on occasion for domestic political reasons. But the stakes in East-West relations are so high—world peace, billions of dollars to be saved or expended in a continuation of the arms race, the internal stability of whole countries—that it seems unwise to jeopardize accord over one problem where both parties may almost see eye-to-eye by dragging in other considerations which, at a minimum, complicate the immediate issue or, going further, put one side's back against the wall. On the other hand, if linkage means looking for complementary trade-offs or sustaining the momentum of East-West bargaining in many domains, this may well facilitate the negotiations on delicate issues.[30]

Should the United States and Western Europe fear that exchange programs and trade will create a truly significant economic challenger sprawling across the Eurasian continent and dominating the world's air and sea lanes as well? If so, should they seek to erect a wall to prevent modernization of the Soviet economy? Both questions are too "iffy." Even if Western governments regarded the first contingency as a significant danger, chances are low for a coordinated blockade lasting for decades. The prospect that the Soviet Union will match and overtake the West economically, moreover, must be regarded as almost visionary. The immediate reality is that the Soviet GNP is equal to about half that of the United States *or* that of Western Europe, taken as a whole. If the trends of recent decades are extrapolated, the picture remains roughly the same for decades to come. The keys to sustained economic growth today are information, technological dynamism, and the ability to apply these assets to production. There is no evident reason why the Western countries should

[30] For more detail, see Clemens, *The Superpowers and Arms Control*, pp. 65–68. For a Soviet critique of "Washington 'Linkages'," see *New Times*, no. 11 (1978), p. 1.

fall behind in these areas. If the Soviet Union makes progress in these realms, the West need not stand still.

In any event, our own problems have more to do with the quality of life and how we distribute and use our wealth rather than with how much we produce. Even if we shift our emphases from quantitative GNP (gross national perspectives) to qualitative concerns, we will surely have sufficient material wealth to maintain whatever modern weaponry is necessary for deterrence.

If Sakharov is correct that the closed nature of the Soviet Union —still a "totalitarian police state, armed wtih superpowerful weaponry"—makes it a greater danger to world peace, this is another incentive for the creation of ties that will open the country so that its citizens know more about the outside world (and each other), and so they and outsiders are less likely to be taken by surprise by actions of the Kremlin.[31] As Solzhenitsyn put it in his Nobel lecture, "within a soundproofed and silenced zone any treaty whatsoever can be reinterpreted at will—or better still, just forgotten."[32] Both men, though differing on many other points, also concur that peace among nations depends upon elimination of violence by governments against their own peoples.

Western analysts and Soviet reformers differ among themselves whether the West should condition its trade and other policies so as to effect internal reform within the Soviet Union—by strengthening one interest group or coalition over another, for example. Solzhenitsyn claims to have become disillusioned and contends that Russians "can obtain freedom only by relying upon [themselves] and that one can place practically no hopes on the West," which props up the Soviet regime by making concessions at an even faster rate than the spiritual regeneration of the Russian people.[33] Sakharov, on the other hand, considers that help from the West has been and will continue to be of great importance in liberalizing Soviet society.

One of the most elaborate analytical frameworks for promoting change in Soviet society has been worked out by Alexander Yanov.[34]

---

[31] Andrei D. Sakharov, *O strane i mire* (New York: Khronika, 1975), p. 71.

[32] *Nobel Lecture* (New York: Farrar, Straus and Giroux, 1972).

[33] See his *Warning to the West* (New York: Farrar, Straus and Giroux, The Noonday Press, 1976), pp. 47, 104–108.

[34] The spectrum of potential contributors to Soviet policy, in Yanov's view, includes a current coalition of (1) the new "new class," headed by the centrists of the Politburo; (2) the local party officials ("little Stalins"); and (3) the military-industrial complex. He fears that the latter two groups will coalesce with (4) the nationalistic neo-Slavophile types and urges instead that Western policies be oriented to form a coalition of the new "new class" with (5) technocrats and (6) liberal intellectuals. See, for example, Yanov, *Détente after Brezhnev*, p. 15.

While sympathizing with Yanov's goals and some of his recommendations, I believe that he overrates the West's ability to understand the Soviet scene, act coherently upon such understanding as exists, act so as to achieve the results desired, and prescribe what is good for the Soviet Union. Programs such as he suggests also evoke the danger of U.S. self-righteousness and moral crusading and the companion danger of Kremlin intransigence if Soviet leaders feel they are being pressured unduly. Solzhenitsyn, at the other extreme, seems to understate the impact that Western influence has already had—even on his own destiny (expulsion rather than another *gulag* or a grave). I would tend to trust more in the long-term serendipitous and synergistic effects on *both* sides of enhanced East-West exchanges, even though they were not so heavily conditioned on particular linkages or directed to particular audiences as some reformers have advocated.[35]

I conclude that, on balance, Western as well as Soviet interests will probably gain from enhancing the foundation of détente and trade between East and West. This is so even though the burden of the arms race falls more heavily on the Soviet Union, and Soviet interests in East-West trade seem to outweigh American interests. Both sides depend upon one another and on themselves to avoid nuclear destruction. East-West transactions can be channeled so as to add to the prospects of peace, lower the price of security, contribute to the common fund of knowledge, enhance the common environment, and add to the repository of culture available to individuals on each side.

If one considers the long-term perspective, one finds that policies rooted in a consistent effort to identify and enhance objectives of all parties concerned have a better prospect of optimizing the particular interests of each actor than do exploitative policies; narrow self-seeking, history suggests, for a time may bring rewards to some individuals, but tends in the long run to be counterproductive for whole societies. (Compare, for example, the rewards in mutual security and prosperity that have flowed from the European Recovery Plan—stimulated between 1948 and 1951 by about $14 billion in transfers from the United States to Europe—with the net gains and liabilities to Moscow from its withdrawal of some $14 to $20 billion in goods and materials from Eastern Europe between 1945 and the mid-1950s.[36]

---

[35] As Soviet dissident Lev Kopelev has argued, the United States should be firm in its convictions "but at the same time offer some golden bridges. Make it so our side can come to you without losing prestige" (*Washington Post*, April 15, 1977).

[36] On "Soviet Economic Policy in Eastern Europe," see Paul Marer in *Reorientation and Commercial Relations of the Economies of Eastern Europe*, submitted to U.S. Congress, Joint Economic Committee (Washington, D.C., 1974), pp. 135–63 at pp. 144–45.

Washington, by its efforts, gained reliable allies and solid trading partners, while Moscow was left with a network of disgruntled and sometimes insurrectionist vassal-states whose capacity to compete economically in world markets has been dreadfully constricted.)

Though zero-sum policies may seem to pay off for a time (at least for some portions of society) before inducing costly counteroffensives by the exploited party, this period grows ever shorter because of the escalating interdependencies and linkages of today's world. As in laboratory runs of "prisoner's dilemma" games, so in world affairs, both narrow self-seeking and unrestrained altruism are counterproductive.[37] These conclusions, if valid, mean that it is generally in the interests of the CEMA and OECD countries to collaborate not only in East-West but in North-South relations.

Nudging toward Globalism

Can it be mutually advantageous for countries of the CEMA, the West, and the Third World to work together more closely in multinational, transnational arenas? By definition this would bind all of us in a more complex web of mutual sensitivity and perhaps vulnerability. To take part, the Eastern states would have to reduce the state-centered quality of their organization and modes of operation. To compete, they would have to become more efficient; if they became more efficient, they would become richer; but to become more efficient, they would probably have to become freer. In this case, the Grand Inquisitor's dichotomy—"Bread or Freedom?"—may not hold; the two might well go together. Whether Brezhnev's successors will want bread at this price is not at all certain.

Not only does the economic and social structure of the countries having developed market economies make them the center for most transnational activity, their prevailing pluralistic ideologies provide much more legitimacy for such activities than is available in Communist countries or many less developed states. But if transnationalism has become the ideology of many rich actors—both corporations and states—nationalism remains the gospel of many poor ones. Since many new states see transnational processes as remnants of colonial rule, nationalists try to diminish transnational ties.[38] Moscow, for its own reasons, is tempted to manipulate these nationalist sentiments so

[37] Unrestrained altruism invites abuse. As Karl W. Deutsch has put it, "both martyrs and cynics will do poorly" in the game of prisoner's dilemma and, by extension, in world politics. See his *The Analysis of International Politics* (Englewood Cliffs, N.J.: Prentice-Hall, 1968), p. 122.

[38] See Nye and Keohane, *Transnational Relations and World Politics*, pp. 387–388.

as to cause relations between countries of the Third World and the West to deteriorate. If the Soviet Union becomes more deeply enmeshed in multilateral and transnational associations with the West, the Kremlin's desire or ability to play this card will probably diminish.

Ideally, solutions to the problems of global interdependence should be rooted in a philosophy of mutual aid, one that works to enhance the long-range interests of all concerned rather than maximizing the immediate goals of those with the most leverage today. The United States can gain important advantages from exploiting its agricultural resources and advanced technology; Saudi Arabia, its oil; Australia and the Soviet Union, their rich mineral resources; and so on. Indeed, groups of nations and transnational corporations can exploit their leverage as principal suppliers or buyers of certain goods and services. The problem is, as argued earlier, that exploitation eventually generates a boomerang effect and makes it difficult if not impossible to work out long-term cooperative programs that are most likely to optimize individual as well as collective interests.

Enlightened self-interest therefore dictates that the Western nations take the lead in shaping collaborative solutions to global problems. To the degree that these are indeed solutions to the problems of the West and the Third World, these areas will be less susceptible to Soviet manipulation. On the contrary, if global cooperation appears to succeed, the Kremlin may be persuaded to join rather than spike them or stand aloof.

Third World efforts to obtain a new economic order are likely to persist, with or without Soviet encouragement. If the West can meet these efforts halfway, or better, making interdependence a perceived reality rather than a tactic for exploitation, Soviet carping will fall on deaf ears.

The collaboration of the U.S.S.R. in dealing with problems of planetary interdependence is highly desirable though not absolutely essential in many cases. Many global programs can be conducted by the nations of the OECD and the Third World without the active participation of CEMA. Indeed, progress in halting environmental pollution depends first of all upon the nations of the OECD, since they are the prime users and polluters of global resources. If, working with less developed countries, they can perfect technologies that generate economic growth and improve environmental standards, such approaches will probably be welcomed in most countries of the Third World.

Global programs should be organized so as to keep the door open for East European and Soviet cooperation. On the other hand, the countries of the West and the Third World should not permit their own cooperation to become contingent upon Soviet participation unless it is absolutely vital. Where Soviet cooperation is essential—in keeping track of world grain stocks and harvests, for example—the West should use the strongest inducements available to ensure Moscow's participation. OECD nations, for example, might condition their own grain sales to the U.S.S.R. on Soviet cooperation in efforts to assure global grain reserves.

Western policy makers should be on guard against zero-sum policies emanating from Moscow, even while trying to persuade Soviet leaders and common citizens that greater collaboration may be in their mutual interest. Since such collaboration may indeed be dictated by life itself, the Soviet elite may come increasingly to realize the futility of zero-sum exploitation and look for outcomes advantageous to all sides. What they rationalize as a tactic of interdependence could eventually become a program.

While the question *kto kovo?* has been emphasized by hardliners on all sides, Soviet spokesmen have also championed another wordplay: *miru mir*—"peace to the world." If Moscow and Washington could replace attitudes of *kto kovo* with a spirit of reciprocity they might better assure *miru mir*.

If these premises are accepted, Westerners—in governmental, educational, economic, and cultural spheres—should seek out their counterparts in countries of CEMA and search for

- new forms of collaboration, feasible for both sides and mutually advantageous
- projects based on the premise of long-term cooperation giving individuals and institutions on both sides a stake in peace and commerce between East and West
- areas where the strengths of the countries of CEMA and the OECD complement one another
- spheres where functional cooperation can develop habits of trust and cooperation with minimal political static
- projects which not only may be advantageous to Easterners and Westerners but which, in a spirit of mutuality, are deemed by countries or firms of the Third World to interest them as well.

As Gvishiani has put it, "the development of cooperation between socialist countries and Western industrial corporations makes the creative search for new organizational forms inevitable," including "new forms of joint ventures which could be acceptable to both partners."[39]

Similarly, Dr. Margarita Inozemtsev has stated that the Soviet Union is ready, in principle, for joint ventures with Western firms and that the obstacles, such as central planning versus individual firms, are frequently institutional. These obstacles can be overcome, however, as they have been overcome by West Germans, for example, by working through Soviet Chambers of Commerce. New mechanisms are needed, she said.[40]

East European states may take the lead in such ventures, as in Rumania's arrangements with Britain and West Germany to produce new aircraft that may compete in CEMA as well as in world markets, and in Hungarian-Swiss collaboration in Nigeria's pharmaceutical industry.[41]

Among East European states, only Yugoslavia is associated with the European Economic Community, but all East European members of CEMA except East Germany belong to the General Agreement on Tariffs and Trade (GATT). Rumania also belongs to the International Monetary Fund and the World Bank.[42] They may help drag the Soviet Union toward multilateralism.[43]

If we press ahead and look for new forms of cooperation, advantageous to all parties concerned, projects that seemed unthinkable yesterday may appear natural tomorrow. Not only does Western Europe get a large fraction of its natural gas requirements from the Soviet Union, for example, as part of a larger deal with Iran, but two-thirds of Europe's enriched uranium in 1976 came on contract from the Soviet Union, which received much of the original ore from the United States—a $220 million "enrichment" business annually for

---

39 Dr. Gvishiani's 1973 San Francisco address, cited above.

40 Dr. Inozemtsev added that with greater familiarity with the Soviet scene, Westerners might learn that more flexibility is possible in the last year or two of a Five-Year Plan; during the initial years, human and other resources are tight. Remarks at the Kennan Institute, May 20, 1977.

41 Rumania signed far-reaching agreements in several fields with American, British, and French firms in 1977 as well as with the West German–Dutch VFW Fokker Company. But President Ceauşescu warned that any U.S. pressure on emigration or other human rights issues could scuttle existing U.S.-Rumanian accords. See *Christian Science Monitor*, July 27, 1977, p. 26.

42 See John P. Hardt et al., *Western Investment in Communist Economies*, prepared for the U.S. Senate, Subcommittee on Multinational Corporations of the Committee on Foreign Relations (Washington, D.C., 1974), p. 36.

43 According to Harold Berman (personal communication), Hungarian and other East European representatives have expressed a strong interest in joint projects with Western organizations in the Third World in meetings of the United Nations Conference on Trade and Development (UNCTAD).

the Soviet Union.[44] The Soviet Union has become a source of Europe's energy supplies not only in league with her southern neighbor, Iran, but also with the other superpower.

Cases of East-West collaboration in the Third World are not common, but Soviet banks are reported to be joining international consortia with Western financial institutions to finance underwriting projects in the Third World.[45] U.S. and Soviet smallpox teams have worked together in the Third World. The Soviet Union and the United States have begun to participate jointly in power projects in third countries such as Colombia and Canada.[46] Whether such instances remain isolated exceptions to a rule or part of a broader movement only time will tell. With more experience on all sides, we may learn how to optimize common interests, not just in commercial affairs, but in many spheres, from physical survival to spiritual enrichment.

Similar conclusions were reached by a Trilateral Commission task force examining the prospects for collaboration in solving global problems between the Trilateral countries (Western Europe, Japan, North America) and Communist states (mainly the U.S.S.R. and China).[47] The study concluded that such cooperation could make an important contribution to coping with substantive problems without undue risk or intrusion into the internal affairs of participating countries. Four areas were judged to be relatively promising:

(1) *Development of an international system of national food reserves.* The reserves would seek to keep cereal price changes within a less disruptive range than in the recent past and to ensure that adequate food supplies were available to developing nations at manageable prices. The U.S.S.R. belongs to the International Wheat Council and could benefit from a system assuring Soviet access to the world market at lower costs than those entailed in building up an autonomous national reserve. But Soviet behavior to date led the task force to conclude that Moscow's participation is unlikely "unless the Tri-

---

[44] *Washington Star,* May 24, 1977, p. A-3. See also *The Nuclear Antiproliferation Act of 1977,* Hearings and Markup before the Committee on International Relations, House of Representatives (Washington, D.C. 1977).

[45] See also Jozef Wilczynski, *The Multinationals and East-West Relations: Towards Transideological Collaboration* (Boulder, Colo.: Westview Press, 1976).

[46] Joint Communique of the Eleventh Dartmouth Conference between U.S. and Soviet representatives in Jurmala, Latvian S.S.R., July 9–13, 1977, in *New Times,* no. 30 (July 1977), pp. 30–31.

[47] *Collaboration with Communist Countries in Managing Global Problems.* Efforts by representatives of the task force to arrange a series of consultations with Soviet and Chinese experts at various stages in the study were unsuccessful.

lateral countries are . . . prepared to proceed in setting up a reserve, without the U.S.S.R. if necessary." Chinese participation in this endeavor, while desirable, was judged "not essential to any reserve scheme, and . . . unlikely to occur."[48]

(2) *International controls over exports of nuclear fuels and processing facilities to make the world less dangerous for all concerned.* In recent London meetings of nuclear fuel suppliers the Soviets have indicated a willingness a take part in such programs. Indeed, differences between Moscow and Washington have often been less acute than among Trilateral states.

(3) *Orderly management of oceanic problems such as fishing, mineral extraction, and pollution.* The Soviet Union, with a vast coastline but also with large distant-water fishing and naval fleets, has a similar mix of interests and has cooperated closely with the United States, Japan, Britain, and France in United Nations Law of the Sea negotiations.[49] If these negotiations produce a treaty, Soviet participation will be needed in its implementation; if the talks break down, the developed countries including the U.S.S.R. will need to set broad norms of conduct for themselves, for example, an acceptable regime for a 200-mile economic zone.

(4) *An internationally negotiated set of trade rules and procedures for arbitrating trade disputes.* Such norms are important because of the rising volume of East-West trade and the special problems entailed in transactions between market and state-controlled economies. The history of U.S.-Soviet trade negotiations in the 1970s has already shown that bilateralism will not protect the Soviet Union from pressure on such matters as human rights that have little to do with external economic relations. And there is no evidence that the Kremlin believes membership in an international economic organization would curtail such demands. Soviet participation in GATT is not essential, and new forms of East-West monetary cooperation are unlikely; but Trilateral countries might well condition their bilateral agreements with CEMA countries on acceptance of an internationally negotiated set of procedures for arbitrating trade disputes.

---

[48] The most promising area for Chinese participation was judged to be earthquake forecasting.

[49] Despite inhibitions on all sides, Soviet and Cuban experts had been issued, and had accepted, invitations to an international marine conference held in Trinidad and Tobago in January 1978. They did not attend, however, because visas were not issued in time. Government officials in Port of Spain were willing to issue courtesy visas, but did not obtain the names of the Soviet participants until two days before the seminar was to begin. Two Cubans were also caught in "the unfortunate state of affairs." *Trinidad Guardian*, January 18, 1978, p. 13. Analogous problems have plagued U.S.-Soviet exchanges for years.

Energy production in the Soviet Union and China could be enhanced by capital and technology imported from Trilateral countries, in exchange for Soviet and Chinese energy exports. Already Soviet oil shipments to Western Europe rival those from Russia to Eastern Europe. West European experience suggests that the problems in such exchanges are manageable so long as dependence on Soviet supplies is kept within prudent limits. But the United States is reluctant to invest scarce resources in a potentially hostile area, while Japan limits its cooperation with Moscow to avoid offending Peking.

More East-West cooperation in development assistance to the Third World is desirable, the task force concluded, but unlikely. The volume of Soviet aid has diminished in recent years (except in the military field), and Soviet manipulation of aid programs for short-term political aims makes international coordination almost impossible. Communist participation in multilateral programs might be enhanced if they were directed explicitly to humanitarian aid to the poorest countries or to boost food production.

Soviet and Chinese participation in international space programs and weather modification and forecasting efforts have proceeded guardedly. Long-term benefits from cooperation in these domains could be useful to all sides, but short-term prospects are limited by technical as well as political obstacles.

In the same vein as the present study, the Trilateral study group concluded that the most likely Soviet policy is "more of the same"—growing imports of trade and technology, against a mixed background of political cooperation and competition. More Soviet participation in globalist endeavors will depend upon the advent to power of leaders more pragmatic and less ideological than the present regime; less anxious to project influence into the Third World; more willing to cut military spending; and more willing to permit a greater degree of pluralism in Eastern Europe and the U.S.S.R.

An East-West Dilemma

While taking account of the dangers to both sides of enhanced interdependence between East and West, this analysis has come down on the side of qualified optimism, especially in the long run, arguing that the realities of today's world make it in the enlightened self-interest of all parties to shape their interactions in mutually beneficial directions. Any balanced and realistic appraisal must also take account of important problems that lie on the horizon today and tomorrow. The root dilemma pervading this analysis is: What are the appropriate trade-offs between Western and Soviet interests in interdependence and security—both domestic and external?

The difficulty in establishing the desirable limits to any exchanges was underscored in July 1977 when the U.S. Department of Commerce rejected a request by the Control Data Corporation for permission to sell a Cyber 76 computer to the Soviet Union—ostensibly for use in a United Nations–sponsored worldwide weather-forecasting system. An earlier model, the Cyber 74, is the central brain of the U.S. defense system and might be adapted to play an important role in the Soviet military and intelligence operations.[50]

Difficult cases of this kind may be interpreted as warnings about how far it is possible or useful to go in trying to expand Western ties with the Soviet Union. But they may also be seen in the context of the longer time frame and philosophical perspective advocated by Dr. Gvishiani:

> Since the U.S.S.R. and U.S.A. have lived in virtual commercial isolation from each other fifty years or more, it should come as no surprise that the build-up of trade, like the build-up of any vast industrial or commercial venture, will take time before it gains momentum. We still have to learn to work together, we have to come to understand systems, procedures and business techniques in our respective countries. In other words, we have to live through a "learner's curve," and one might compare this curve to that of a large commercial jet requiring a very long runway and lengthy taxiing on the ground before it is airborne, but once airborne, the climb and the speed are swift.[51]

Though East and West may learn to work more smoothly, and a deepening of bilateral and even global ties may in the long run be seen as beneficial by most Western and Soviet citizens, top leaders of the CPSU may nonetheless regard this process as damaging to their regime. How the Kremlin views its problems of domestic security thus generates hard choices for all parties. If closer ties between East and West deepen the pressures for liberalization within Eastern Europe or the Soviet Union, what should the Western response be? Should the West use its enhanced leverage to condition détente and trade upon Soviet respect for human rights—or should it assume a

---

[50] *Time*, August 1, 1977, pp. 42–45. On the context of such problems, see U.S. Congress, House of Representatives, Committee on International Relations, *Science, Technology, and American Diplomacy: An Extended Study of the Interactions of Science and Technology with United States Foreign Policy*, 3 vols. (Washington, D.C., 1977), especially vol. 3.

[51] Gvishiani, address at the International Industrial Conference.

posture of noninterference in the domestic affairs of others? Just as instabilities in the Third World and the West may tempt Soviet intervention, so Western policy makers have to weigh the benefits of détente and trade against the prospects of helping to generate a more democratic and humane rule in the Soviet sphere. No serious statesman would risk a major war for more democracy in Eastern Europe or the Soviet Union, but what if Western support for liberalization in the Soviet sphere risks only a decline in East-West trade or some acceleration of the arms race? If the sphere of human rights can be uncoupled from trade and arms control, as President Carter has attempted to do, Western objectives might be pursued in each area without dangerous overlap. But if Western influences threaten the domestic tranquility of the socialist camp, the Kremlin will assert linkage whether Washington does so or not.

The West is left with a moral problem: How far to push for liberalization if this may undermine Moscow's commitment to détente and trade and, a fortiori, to global collaboration? Perhaps the Kremlin will eventually be persuaded that its best interests would not be unduly threatened and might even prosper through liberalization in Eastern Europe and at home. Before Moscow accepts this view, however, shrimps may learn to whistle. Even if espoused by the Kremlin, a strategy of liberalization might well yield a series of convulsions likely to set back the clock in a reactionary direction.

But Soviet policy making is not monolithic; it is the result of competition among different individuals, interest groups, bureaucracies, generations, and nationalities. Enlightened Western policies may strengthen the hands of those dedicated to exploring new modes of East-West and global cooperation. Although political change within the Soviet Union could damp the Kremlin's interest in collaboration between East and West, it could also open the door to new opportunities.

Time, toleration, and thermonuclear terror have given both sides the opportunity to shift their relationship from cold war to a structure of peace rooted in a sense of interdependence—strategic, economic, technological, and ecological.

Slowly but surely the lesson sinks in: In an age of escalating interdependencies, no man and no state are islands unto themselves; each is a part of the main. And what Adam Smith once said about the nation pertains to the globe: So long as any part of the body politic is undernourished, the health of the whole cannot flourish.

Nonetheless, interdependence and/or security will likely remain a dilemma for Western as well as Soviet leaders for years to come.

INDEX

INDEX

Cover and book design: Pat Taylor